EDGAR CAYCE, the twentieth century's most astoundingly accurate prophet, had the psychic gift of being able to put himself into a state of self-induced trance. In this state, Cayce, a man of little formal education and not scholarly by temperament, predicted such future events as the discovery of the Dead Sea Scrolls and the development of the laser beam. He was also capable of diagnosing illnesses that were beyond the knowledge of contemporary physicians—often for people thousands of miles away.

But outstanding among all his accomplishments as a clairvoyant, mystic and prophet was his ability—through psychic readings as well as in his life teachings—to make the Bible live!

Here are Edgar Cayce's magnificent revelations about God, Reincarnation and the true meaning of the Old Testament . . .

A MILLION YEARS TO THE PROMISED LAND

A MILLION YEARS TO THE PROMISED LAND

Edgar Cayce's Story of the Old Testament Genesis through Deuteronomy

ROBERT W. KRAJENKE

A NATIONAL GENERAL COMPANY

A MILLION YEARS TO THE PROMISED LAND
A Bantam Book / published September 1973

Library of Congress Cataloging in Publication Data

Krajenke, Robert W
    A million years to the Promised Land.

    1. Bible and spiritualism. 2. Cayce, Edgar,
1877–1945.   I. Cayce, Edgar, 1877–1945.   II. Title.
BF1311.B5K7   222'.1'06   73–10183

Published simultaneously in the United States and Canada

Bantam Books are published by Bantam Books, Inc., a National
General company. Its trade-mark, consisting of the words "Bantam
Books" and the portrayal of a bantam, is registered in the United
States Patent Office and in other countries. Marca Registrada.
Bantam Books, Inc., 666 Fifth Avenue, New York, N. Y. 10019.

PRINTED IN THE UNITED STATES OF AMERICA

DEDICATED
TO ALL THOSE
WHO ARE A PART
OF THIS STORY

And is there a nation on the earth like thy people Israel, whom God saved to be a people for himself and to make him a name and to do for him great and notable deeds upon the earth, as he had done in former days for thy people whom thou savedst for thyself out of Egypt, a people whose God thou art?　　　　　　　　　　　　*2 Samuel 7:23*

For the universe, God, is within. Thou art His. Thy communion with the cosmic forces of nature, thy communion with thy Creator, is thy birthright! Be satisfied with nothing less than walking with Him.　　　　　　　　　　　　*(1297-1)*

Contents

FOREWORD ix

INTRODUCTION xi

Chapter 1
IN GOD'S MIND
A SPIRITUAL CREATION 1

Chapter 2
THE COMING OF ADAM 23

Chapter 3
THE FALL OF MAN 45

Chapter 4
CAIN AND ABEL:
HOSTILE BROTHERS 55

Chapter 5
THE DELUGE:
DIVISION AND DISSENT 73

Chapter 6
THE TOWER OF BABEL 97

Chapter 7
ABRAHAM, ISAAC, AND JACOB 103

Chapter 8
JOSEPH: FORERUNNER
OF THE CHRIST 141

Chapter 9
EXODUS 151

THE RELEVANCE AND SIGNIFICANCE
OF THE PHENOMENA AND PHILOSO-
PHY OF EDGAR CAYCE'S TODAY 253

RECOMMENDED READING 255

Foreword

Several hundred people, of the twenty-five hundred who had Life Readings from Edgar Cayce, were told that they had incarnations in Biblical times.

From early childhood Edgar Cayce was a devout Bible student and began teaching Sunday School, using the standard orthodox literature, while still in his teens. He continued this practice throughout his life. Many are still living who remember his outstanding ability as a Bible teacher, most of whom never knew him as a psychic or in any other capacity than as a teacher.

A few years before Edgar Cayce died he was persuaded, by members of several local A.R.E. Study Groups, to teach a weekly interdenominational Bible Class starting with the Book of Genesis and going straight through the Bible.

As a child Edgar Cayce had determined to read the Bible through in a year, by reading three chapters each week-day and five on Sunday. After doing this he decided to read more chapters each day until he could catch up to his years of age. After reaching that point he continued to read the Bible through each year, until—when he died at the age of sixty-seven—he had read the Bible through sixty-seven times!

The Tuesday Night Bible Class, as it was called, wanted Edgar Cayce to incorporate in his teaching not only his own knowledge of the Bible but his understanding of the concepts presented through his psychic readings. The members had already been exposed to some of these concepts through their study of the lessons "in soul development" contained in Books I and II of *A Search for God*.

Having been Edgar Cayce's secretary since 1923, I was asked to take down in shorthand and transcribe the Bible Minutes from these weekly discussions.

Robert Krajenke has shown extraordinary insight in paralleling Edgar Cayce's comments on the Bible, and blending them with the quotes from the Life Readings having to do with Old Testament characters.

It has long been my belief that Edgar Cayce's greatest contribution to this age was his making the Bible come alive for so many people. I saw this happen during his lifetime. Since his death I have seen it even more.

Edgar Cayce loved the Old Testament. He used to say often that without the Old we would not have had the New; without Abraham, Moses, David, we would not have had Jesus.

Now Robert Krajenke, through his discernment and compilation of Edgar Cayce's statements both in the conscious and psychic state, is perhaps again making the Bible live for the many who will read these pages.

Gladys Davis Turner

Introduction

The Bible is a Book of Life, and all Life comes from God. What we find in Scripture we see manifested in our lives every day. Unless we can experience the validity of the concepts presented to us, we have no basis for understanding their merit or meaning. We believe the Bible because we can experience its truths. It is possible to experience everything written in the Bible, Edgar Cayce said, and that is why the Book is holy, and why it comes from God.

Jesus quoted what the psalmist already knew—that we are all gods in the making. (John 10:34; Psalm 82:6) We are gods because we possess a soul. It is the soul that is the Image of God, the readings tell us, and not the physical body. For Edgar Cayce, the Bible was an inspired record, the word of God written by men as they were moved by the Spirit. And what inspired them? Cayce asked. Their souls! We are all potential Christs, and as the Spirit moves through our souls, we can write, read, and live in the same consciousness as the saints and prophets of the past.

The approach of Edgar Cayce is based on application and experience. His interpretations have the unique and vital quality of making the Bible "come alive."

A number of people who knew Edgar Cayce feel that the greatest contribution he made in their lives was to re-awaken them to the Bible. Since his death, many who have studied his psychic legacy have carried the same conviction.

A study of the Cayce interpretations, co-related with regular reading of the Bible, can increase the dimensions of our own humanity as well as make the Divine more real.

The following are a few examples from the clairvoyant discourses of Edgar Cayce regarding the Bible.

Q-7 What present printed version of the Bible gives the nearest to the true meaning of both the New and Old Testaments?
A-7 The nearest true version for the entity is that ye apply of whatever version ye read, in your life. It isn't that ye learn from anyone. Ye only may have the direction. The learning, the teaching is within self. For where hath He promised to meet thee? Within the temple! Where is that temple? Within! Where is heaven on earth? Within! Meet thy Savior there . . .

There have been many versions of that which was purposed to have been written, and has been changed from all of those versions, but remember that the whole Gospel of Jesus Christ is: "Thou shalt love the Lord thy God with all thy mind, thy heart, and thy body, and thy neighbor as thyself." Do this and thou shalt have eternal life. The rest of the book is trying to describe that. It is the same in any language, any version. (2072-14*)

For there be many misinterpretations, poor translations, but to find fault with that thou hast and not used same is to make excuses that you haven't it as it was given . . . (281-20)

For much might be given respecting that ye have that ye call the Bible. This has passed through many hands. Many that would turn that which was written into the meanings that would suit their own purposes, as *ye* yourselves oft do. But if ye will get the spirit of that

*The numbers following verbatim quotes identify the case number as it is cataloged at the library of the Association for Research & Enlightenment, Inc., Virginia Beach, Va.

written there ye may find it will lead thee to the gates of heaven . . . Read it to be wise. Study it to understand. Live it to know that the Christ walks through same with thee. (262–60)

But study and know thy relationship to the Creator. No better handbook may be used than the Scripture itself. (1966–1)

Source Material

The concepts presented in this book are drawn from the clairvoyant readings of Edgar Cayce. A secondary source is the commentary and philosophy he expressed in his weekly Bible class.

The Readings

Edgar Cayce had the psychic gift of being able to put himself into a self-induced trance. While in this state, Cayce was completely unconscious, yet able to discourse at length on any subject which was asked of him. Although a man of little formal education, and not scholarly by temperament, while in this sleep-like condition, Cayce had access to unlimited information.

These discourses are called "readings."

The accuracy of many of the readings can be ascertained because they related to the diagnosis of physical ailments, often for people hundreds or thousands of miles away, whom Cayce had never met or seen.

Still other readings contained intimations of the future which have been confirmed by the passage of time. The readings anticipated such events as the discovery of the laser beam and gave vivid descriptions of an Essene community before the discovery of the Dead Sea Scrolls.

The approach to Life taken by the readings, with its emphasis on dreams, meditation, and small group dynamics, is clearly a harbinger of many recent developments, and several decades ahead of the interest now shown by psychologists, theologians, and social therapists. In many ways, the readings' view on the nature of Man and the possibilities in Life are still far ahead of the conclusions and implications drawn by these modern practitioners.

The readings also discussed reincarnation and dealt with it in a specific framework compatible with Judeo-Christian ethics. Indeed, reincarnation aids in clarifying many of the enigmatic and mysterious statements made throughout Scripture.

The framework, philosophy, and logic of reincarnation, as explained by Edgar Cayce, give a consistent picture of God's Love and also offer an acceptable explanation of Jesus' life and development as the Savior. It was the result of many incarnations in the earth in which all the trials and errors of the flesh were experienced and overcome by the soul's yearning to be One with God.

Perhaps what is most inspiring and encouraging about a Bible with reincarnation in it is that we may find ourselves as part of the story, as many who obtained readings from Edgar Cayce did.

The discourses which deal directly with reincarnation are called "Life Readings," and were given for individuals who requested them. They described influences from previous incarnations which were directly affecting the present life of the individual.

In many instances Biblical incarnations were given, and, in this volume, are a primary source of information. All extracts from the readings are verbatim quotes.

Cayce said the source of his information came from the knowledge and memory stored in the subconscious mind of the individual for whom the reading was given. If this is correct, and his descriptions of past lives accurate, the Life Readings are as close as we can come to actual "eye-witness" accounts. These readings are a unique and fascinating record of the thoughts, the emotions, the effects of circumstance upon the consciousness of individuals who were present when the Old Testament history was being lived.

Almost all the readings which Cayce gave show the influence of the Bible, yet few readings were devoted exclusively to Scripture.

The 364 series contains 12 discourses devoted to the history of Atlantis and the symbology of Genesis. The 281 series contains 65 discourses dealing with healing prayer and a study of the Revelation of St. John. The 5749 series was obtained by Tom Sugrue for his philosophy chapter in *There Is a River*, and contains some of the best exposition of the Cayce philosophy paralleled with Christian theology and the tenets of other religious beliefs. The 262 series of 130 discourses deals with the principles of spiritual growth, and forms the basis of the *A Search for God* program of the Association for Research & Enlightenment, Inc.

These series contain the best material for interpreting a clairvoyant's view of the great themes and questions which are raised in Scripture, such as the nature of God and His relationships to Man; the purpose for life in the earth, and why Man loves and why he suffers; Good and Evil, Karma and Grace, Free Will and Predestination.

The Bible Class

The second source of Edgar Cayce's interpretations of the Bible is the record kept in his Tuesday Night Bible Class which he conducted during the last four years of his life.

Edgar Cayce was born and raised in a Fundamentalist tradition. In the early days, his career as a psychic offered him no major theological difficulties. He was able to diagnose physical ailments, and the people recovered when his recommendations were applied. His strange gift seemed to be simply a manifestation of God's Love.

But as his work continued and his fame grew, requests began coming in from a variety of people in widely scattered environments, and concepts such as reincarnation and astrology began appearing in his discourses.

Cayce, who never recalled a word he spoke in trance, was troubled by the presence of these unorthodox concepts. For a long time he debated if he should continue giving readings. Yet the conflict was finally resolved. "No one seemed to be getting hurt," he observed, "and the readings are still doing good." Thus, God's Love was still working in mysterious ways its wonders to perform.

And it caused Edgar Cayce to think, to study the readings, and to discuss them with those who were close to him.

As Cayce matured and developed, his unconscious statements became fully integrated into his conscious philosophy.

Although a lifelong Bible class teacher, his Tuesday Night class, coming at the end of his life, represents some of his most developed perceptions.

The Bible was not studied as a history or past fact. The lives of the Bible characters and the conditions which surrounded them were studied as relative conditions, stages of development, or planes of consciousness which were applicable in the present. Not only were the great accomplishments studied, but also the faults and failures, in order to make the Bible characters more real and understandable.

The main objective of the study was to gain a better concept of the Bible and its personal relationship to each individual, and to determine which truths were applicable in daily life.

No claim is made that these quotes reflect the actual words spoken by Edgar Cayce. Indeed, what was recorded was often the consensus of opinion following a group discussion over which Cayce presided. In presenting these quotes, I have felt free to edit and rework the material in order to present it as succinctly as possible.

It was Edgar Cayce's intention to review all the material upon completion of the study and make any necessary additions or changes before allowing publication. He died before the study reached its conclusion. Thus, the Bible notes have never been widely circulated.

Overview
From Genesis To The Revelation

For students of the Edgar Cayce readings, the two key books of the Bible are Genesis and The Revelation.

"Unless you understand The Revelation," Cayce once said, "you can't understand the Bible. And you can't understand The Revelation until you understand Genesis."

In The Beginning God created the heavens and the earth. (Genesis 1:1)

Genesis begins with a simple premise. God is *Spirit*, and Life both in the heavens and of the earth, in all its phases and expressions, is a manifestation of that power.

God is. God was. He ever shall be. With God there is no beginning.

Then, to what does "The Beginning" refer?

The earth is just one aspect of God's total creativity. Our planet is just a mote in our solar system, and our solar system is a speck in a larger system, which in turn is only a part of something even greater—a universe within universes!

"The Beginning" is not a description of God's first creative act, nor even of His most important. "The Beginning" describes that creation in which Man—God's child—finds himself.

According to Edgar Cayce, the purpose of Genesis was to keep in the mind of man a memory of "The Beginning."

". . . for as is seen, that as is given [in Genesis] is the presentation of a teacher of a peoples that separated for that definite purpose of keeping alive in the minds, the hearts, the *soul*-minds of entities, that there may be seen their closer relationships to the divine influences of Creative Forces, that brought into being all that appertains to man's indwelling as man in the form of flesh in this material world." (364–5)

Additional information in the Cayce readings states the substance of Genesis was drawn from extant, ancient manuscripts, and from information Moses obtained while in deep states of meditation. Other references indicate Joshua, Moses' aide, possessed psychic powers and assisted in the interpretation of both the psychic and historical materials.

Moses, as the author of Genesis, was attempting to give an all-inclusive description of Creation and the place man had in it.

Genesis affirms Man was created in the Image of God, which the readings interpreted to be the soul, not the physical body. Man, according to Edgar Cayce, was first a celestial being in a spiritual world. Only through a Fall, a rebellion in heaven, did man become a material being. The spiritual estate was lost to the flesh.

Moses was recounting the evolution of God's Spirit in the earth, telling the story in a highly condensed, symbolic language through which the finite mind of the Israelites could grasp an understanding of infinite happenings.

Just as Genesis preserves a past memory, The Revelation points to potential consciousness.

"And then The Revelation . . . is a description of, a possibility of, thy own consciousness, and not as a historical fact, not as a fancy, but as that thy own soul has sought throughout its experiences, through the phases of thy abilities, the faculties of the mind and body, the emotions of all thy complex . . . system." (1473–1)

The Revelation is the restoration of John's consciousness of himself as a spiritual being. The first eleven chapters of The Revelation deal with experiences through dream and meditation regarding the purification of John's body and subconscious mind. The remaining chapters show the affects. The flesh no longer binds him nor limits his consciousness. John obtained that state promised by The Christ—"a memory before the foundations of the world." John was conscious of that estate he shared with God "In The Beginning" as a soul before the world was made, or Genesis was written.

Between Genesis and Revelation is the history of a nation, the first of which we have a record, who chose One God and experienced everything that is possible to be experienced in this earth. There were other groups who believed in one God, but only the chronicles of the Jews present a complete and continuous history, with the good and the evil, the beautiful and the immoral running together. It describes their beliefs, and what they did about them. From Genesis to Revelation there is presented a complete pattern of man's experience in the earth. The pattern visible throughout the Bible is a viable one through which all men can obtain that condition realized by John.

Prologue

Pre-Existence in the Light and the Fall from Grace

When was "The Beginning?" It was when consciousness began, as seen from this answer from the question:

Q–4 When did I first exist as a separate entity?
A–4 . . . the first existence . . . was in the *Mind* of the Creator, as all souls became a part of the creation. As to time, this would be in the beginning. When was the beginning? First consciousness! (2925–1)

Man's first awareness was spiritual. Man's first existence was as a celestial being in God's Mind. God is Spirit, and Man, in His image, was a spiritual creation.

Many are the Cayce readings which strongly and beautifully affirm that the gift of Free Will is inherent in this creation, and is the birthright and heritage of each soul.

God desired companionship, and in His desire moved in spirit and brought co creators, heirs to the Kingdom—the Sons of God—into existence.

All God's creations follow fixed laws and will always be that which they were set to be in the beginning, except Man. A star will never be a moon, nor a moon a rose, nor a rose a man. Only Man can—and did—rebel against God, and thus altered his destiny.

The consciousness of the Light was followed by chaos. In Genesis 1:2, Darkness covers the face of the Deep. What is deeper than God? or darker than sin? This verse indicates the condition which resulted as souls began to misuse and abuse their birthright of Will, and first occurred in spirit, before the earth was made.

The loss of the First Consciousness, or Divine Awareness, was the result of rebellion. The spirit of selfishness is symbolized in Lucifer, Satan, the Devil, and the Serpent. They all are one—spiritual rebellion.

Separated from the source of Light and Love, many of the Sons of God became oblivious to the purpose for which they were created. The Father knew if they continued in their activities, ultimately they would deteriorate all their spiritual glory and power, and efface their own existence.

The truest utterance in all Scripture, which Cayce stressed, is "God does not will that any soul should perish." (2 Peter 3:9)

The earth was first an expression of God and not intended as a place of habitation for souls, yet it became the place of opportunity through which these spirits could realize their separation. The pain, the adversity and suffering of material existence would eventually awaken within the soul the unquenchable desire to return to God. The parable of the Prodigal Son is a model of this experience.

Throughout its long stages of evolution, souls were fascinated with the material creation, and tempted by the possibilities in it for expression and experience. Unspeakable conditions began to manifest as a result of their interference with natural laws. Much of mythology, with its monsters, centaurs, harpies, gods, and heroes, consists of memories of this earliest, pre-Adamic history.

Because God is love, and wills no soul perish, a divine plan was instituted. In order to establish a standard, or means of comparison by which these souls, entrapped in their own distorted thought-creation, or ego-projections, could measure themselves against perfection, God made himself manifest through the creature called Adam, or Man.

The Divine Image appeared in physical form through Adam who was the prototype for a race which appeared in the earth in five places at once. Sons of God, who were still in spiritual surroundings and conscious of the Light, chose to take on the form of Man, and entered into the earth and began a ministry of love, education, and healing to their brothers.

The soul whom we know as Jesus was the leader and director of this movement, and is the one we know as the first Adam.

The work of the five lines of the Adamic race was nothing less than the resuscitation of imperfect man and the regeneration of his fallen consciousness, a work which still continues.

The Fall of Adam is representational of the fall in flesh of the perfect race. They also were tempted by the possibilities for experience in a material world. Eventually they lost the consciousness of their spiritual ideal and purpose for entering the world. From time to time great leaders arose to remind them that the kingdom they were seeking was a spiritual one and not earthly.

It was over two hundred thousand years between the first experience of Adam and the last as Jesus. Other lives in the Old Testament of this soul include those as Enoch, Melchizedek, Joseph, Joshua, and Jeshua, highpriest following the return from Babylon. An incarnation as Asaph, choirmaster at the time of King David, is intimated. The readings suggest other incarnations as well—a total of 33. In all of them, the Master-soul contributed the knowledge of "The Lord, Thy God, is One" to all religions.

Summary:

A Million Years To The Promised Land

Time and *Space* are elusive entities, difficult to describe and impossible to contain in one definition. Man's ideas about Time and Space change in each age, and every individual has had some subjective experience in which a minute or a mile has taken on different colorations and meanings depending upon circumstances and emotion.

The Cayce readings describe Time as merely as convenience created by man in order to measure and interpret his experiences while in a finite consciousness. In the Mind of God there is no time. A thousand years and a day are the same. According to the readings, Time, Space, and Patience are the three dimensions of Man's consciousness —and through Patience, Time and Space are overcome.

The age Cayce attributed to our planet and the origin of man was startling, and controversial in his day, but in a few decades, modern science has made his dating credible. Scientist Norman Wakefield claims to have discovered animal footprints in Australia 350 million years old. Researcher Richard Leakey claims a human skull found in Tanzania is 2.5 million years old. These dates fit comfortably in Cayce's cosmology.

Cayce described the civilization of Atlantis at length and in great detail, covering a history which stretched across eons.

The Scriptural writers did not share the same concern for Time as does modern man—or even proper chronology. Time is as elusive in the Bible as it is in the readings. An eon, a century, or a decade can be covered in a single chapter without comment or explanation. Everything is ordered around the purpose for the Book being written. Chronology, history, facts, everything is subordinated to the sense and meaning which the writers were trying to convey—who Man was, where he came from and to where he was headed.

Although few theological circles still determine the earth's age from Adam's geneology, they may find Edgar Cayce's story of Adam controversial.

The following verbatim extracts and commentary on Genesis have been arranged, as closely as possible, to follow the Bible text. A continuous history is presented, from the first Creation in the Mind of God—or "First Consciousness"—unto the death of Moses, a period of untold years, preparing for possession of the Holy Ground upon which the Divine Drama of Man's Salvation would be enacted.

Hopefully, the following pages will provide the impetus and foundation for a deeper reading and appreciation of the Old Testament story.

Chapter 1
(Genesis 1)

In God's Mind
A Spiritual Creation

The earth's sphere, with the creation in the mind of the Creator, has kept its same Creative Energy, for God is the same yesterday, today, and forever . . . (900–340)

Hence we find the evolution of the soul, as has been given, and as is manifest in the material world, took place before man's appearance, the evolution of the soul in the mind of the Creator, not in the material world. (900–19)

Genesis 1, according to Edgar Cayce, is the description of a *spiritual* creation, occurring within the Mind of God. All things first originate in Spirit, the readings proclaim. Material existence is a shadow, or reflection, of spiritual patterns. Material evolution is a reflection of a process of God's consciousness as He directed the manifestation of His spirit in materiality.

The earth and the universe, as related to man, came into being through the *Mind—Mind—*of the Maker . . . (900–227)

Mind is ever the builder. For in the beginning, God moved and mind, knowledge, came into being—and the earth and the fullness thereof became the result . . . (5000–1)

1

"God's Mind" is a creative energy, a conscious and intelligent force composed of Love, Harmony and Beauty, and is omnipotent and omnipresent.

According to the interpretation in the Gospel of St. John, the Light which was in Jesus was the same Light out of which the world was created.

. . . Would that all would learn that He, the Christ-consciousness, is the Giver, the Maker, the Creator of the world and all that be therein. (696-3)

The following indicates how early in the process of Creation souls became fascinated and tempted by the possibilities for their own expressions and experiences.

When the earth became a dwelling place for matter, when gases formed into those things that man sees in nature and in activity about him, then matter began its ascent in the various forms of physical evolution—in the *mind* of God!

The spirit chose to enter (celestial, not an earth spirit—he hadn't come into earth yet!), chose to put on, to become a part of that which was as a command not to be done! (262-99)

It was this *spirit* in rebellion that later was represented by the serpent.

Remember, as given, the earth is that speck, that part in creation where souls projected themselves into matter, and thus brought conscious awareness of themselves entertaining the ability of creating without those forces of the spirit of truth.

Hence, that which has been indicated—that serpent, that Satan, that power manifested by entities that . . . through Will separated themselves. (5755-2)

Q-2 In relation to the Oneness of all force, explain the popular concept of the Devil, seemingly substantiated in the Bible by so many passages of Scripture.

A-2 In the beginning, celestial beings. We have first the Son, then the other sons, or celestial beings, that are given their force and power.

Hence that force which rebelled in the unseen forces (*or in spirit*) that came into activity, was that influence which has been called Satan, the Devil, the Serpent; they are One. That of *rebellion*. (262-52)

Hence, "darkness was upon the face of the Deep." This represents the spirit of ignorance, selfishness, the loss of the Divine Awareness which resulted when the Sons of God separated themselves from the Creator.

As the above readings affirm, this occurred in spirit, before the earth was made. The earth, as written, was "without form and void."

As has been given, error or separation began before there appeared what we know as the Earth, the Heavens, or before Space was manifested. (262-115)

"And the spirit of God Moved upon the Face of the Waters"

In the beginning, when chaos existed in the creating of the earth, the Spirit of God moved over the face of same and out of chaos came the world—with its beauty in natural form, or in nature. (3976-8)

The following reading reaffirms the concept which has already been advanced. The creation of matter was first only an expression of God. But it became a source

3

of self-indulgence and selfish expression as His Sons and Daughters began to project their individual and personal influences into it.

For the spirit of God moved and that which is in matter came into being for the opportunities of . . . His Sons, His Daughters. These are ever spoken of as One.

Then came that as sought self-indulgence, self-glorification; and there was the beginning of warring among themselves for activity—STILL in Spirit.

Then those that had made selfish movements moved into that which was and is *Opportunity,* and there came life into same. (262–114)

Thus, in the reading's view, the earth was not created out of a Void or from Nothingness. Rather, His spirit moved over the chaos and rebellion, and from these diverse elements He created Balance and Harmony, and established the foundations of the World.

The World became a place of "Opportunity" through which souls could begin to realize their separation from their spiritual surroundings.

As given from the beginning, by becoming aware in a material world *is*—or was—the only manner or way through which spiritual forces might become aware of their separation from the spiritual atmosphere, the spiritual surroundings of the Maker.

What has been given as the truest of all that has ever been written in Scripture? "God does not will that any soul should perish!" but man, in his head-strongness, harkens oft to that which would separate him from His Maker! (262–56)

Apparently, "The Spirit of God moved upon the Face of the Waters" is correct as a description of the first phase of the material evolution of the earth. As it moved

4

through the Mind of God, its first appearance was as "mist" or vapors.

. . . those portions as man looks up to in space, the mists that are gathering—what's the beginning of this? In this same beginning, so began the earth's sphere. (900–340)

The following is Cayce's description of the entire evolutionary progress.

First that of a mass, about which there arose the mist, and then the rising of same with light breaking *over* that as it *settled* itself as a companion of those in the universe, as it began its *natural* (or now natural) rotations, with the varied effects *upon* the various portions of same, as it slowly—and is slowly—receding or gathering closer to the sun, from which it receives its impetus for the awakening of the elements that give life itself, by [the] radiation of like elements from that which it receives from the sun. (364–6)

How long did this evolution take? How long were the Days of Creation? Seven days? Seven years? Or seven million years or a trillion years? Vast epochs of Time are involved in which spiritual awareness became a material consciousness.

Time is a relative concept devised by man as a means to measure and understand his own experiences. Yet, as Cayce states in one reading, one minute experiencing the consciousness of God is more real and enduring than a thousand years of experience among the carnal-minded.

With the creation of the earth and souls willfully projecting into it, we find two important statements made by Edgar Cayce.

The first is his affirmation that the earth was a

5

separate creation from souls, and not intended as a habitation for them.

The earth and its manifestations were only the expression of God and not necessarily as a place of tenancy for the souls of men, until man was created —to meet the needs of existing conditions. (5749-14)

Cayce's other statement defines the real dwelling place —the universe!

For the universe was brought into being for the purpose of being the dwelling place of the souls of God's children—of which birthright this entity is a part. (2396-2)

"And Dry Land Appeared"

As the earth evolved, continents appeared and oceans formed. The Sons of God experienced each phase of development.

Two states of consciousnesses were being expressed: those who were "Sons of Darkness," who were becoming more and more selfish and material-minded, and those who were still "Children of the Light," who were experiencing the cycles of evolution through the Light and in harmony with God's Patterns.

It is necessary here to follow out the the activities of the Sons of Darkness, in order to establish our premise.

As these souls took on form and shape, great civilizations evolved over the continents. These beings possessed great mental and spiritual powers, and warfare— a reflection of the spiritual pattern—began between the two groups.

The readings admonish us not to confuse our flesh bodies of today with the bodies of Man in the very early history. They were soul-bodies then, Cayce states, "light" bodies which "were not so closely knit in matter." (281–42)

Lecturing to his Bible students, Cayce described the condition thus:

"These beings were male and female in one; they were images (in spirit) of that God-spirit which moved and brought Light into being. Consequently, they also had the ability to push out of themselves, or to divide into various manifestations. They began to do this for their own selfish gratification, or for the propagation of their own selfishness, rather than for the glory of their Creator.

Unless we can get a glimpse of such a state existing in the earth, it will be impossible to understand the necessity, later, of God creating a perfect man, through which all souls might return to their original source."

"And God Said, Let There Be Light"
(Gen. 1:3)

A characteristic of Cayce's interpretations is that all phases of Scripture are related to states of consciousness which are directly experiential.

Thus, "Let there be Light" can be experienced through an awakening to the perfection of the godhead within.

The verse also relates to "First consciousness," and the creation of souls.

For in the beginning, God said, "Let there be light." You are one of those sparks of light, with all the ability of Creation, with all the knowledge of God. (5367 1)

When Jesus spoke of himself as "The Light" it was in reference to this Light of Genesis.

Begin and read Genesis 1:3, and see that is to thee LIGHT, the light of men, even that One who is the Christ-Consciousness. (3660–1)

This verse was of central importance to Edgar Cayce. One of his Bible class students recalls his stating that the rest of Scripture was an attempt to explain, "And God said, Let there be Light."

Apparently the First Consciousness of souls not only partook of the awareness of "The Lord thy God is One," but also "love of neighbor as self":

The SPIRIT moved—or soul moved—and there was Light (Mind). The Light became the light of man—Mind made aware of conscious existence in spiritual aspects or relationships as one to another. (1947-3)

The Divine Image

In Genesis 1:27 it is written, "God created man in His own image." God is Spirit, and therefore the image is spiritual. According to Edgar Cayce, the Divine Image is the soul of man, the *Mind* and *Spirit* those aspects of Man which are god-like, individual, and eternal.

For the image in which man was created is spiritual, as He thy Maker is spiritual. (1257-1)

For the *soul* was made in the image of the Creator, to be a companion with that influence which is constructive, which is creative. (1232-1)

For as each soul—not the body but the soul—is the image of the Maker, so with the awareness of the soul-consciousness there may come the awakening to the realization of the soul's relationship with that universal consciousness, as is promised in Him. (2246-1)

... the *soul* remains ever as one. For it is in the image of the Creator and has its birthright in Him. (1243-1)

This describes the state of man "In The Beginning."

Man in his former state, or natural state, or perma-

8

nent consciousness IS soul. Hence in the beginning all were souls of that creation, with the body as of the Creator—of the spirit forces that make manifest in using same in the various phases or experiences of consciousness for the activity. (262–89)

These two extracts indicate the nature of these pre-Adamic creations:

Some brought about monstrosities, as those of its [that entity's] association by its projection with its association with beasts of various characters. Hence those of the Styx, satyr, and the like; those of the sea, or mermaid; those of the unicorn, and those of the various forms—these projections of what? The abilities of the *psychic* forces (psychic meaning, then, of the mental *and* the soul) . . . (364–10)

. . . there . . . were those who were physically entangled in the animal kingdom with [the] appendages, with cloven hooves, with four legs, with portions of trees, with tails, with scales, with those various things that thought forms (or evil) had so indulged in as to separate the purpose of God's creation of man as man—not as animal . . . (2072 8)

The Pre-Adamic World

Although the mating of the Sons of God with the Daughters of Men is considered a post Adamic experience, Cayce used this verse many times to describe events occuring many thousands of years before Adam.

And it came to pass, when men began to multiply on the face of the earth, and daughters were born unto them,

That the sons of God saw the daughters of men were fair; and they took them wives of all which they chose."
(Genesis 6:1–2)

9

The lust described above was only one form of indulgence. Yet, in essence, it captures the spirit of the whole Rebellion.

. . . as a spirit [man] pushed his individuality into matter and began to express or manifest PERSONAL influence—for self, for ease, for comforts, for those things that would enable the individual entity to, in matter, lord [it] over others. (1448–2)

The following reading is a direct interpretation of the meaning of "Sons of God," and "Daughters of Men."

Q–4 Explain the "Sons of God—Daughters of Men —Sons of Man."
A–4 . . . the influences of those souls that sought material expression pushed themselves into thought forms in the earth. And owing to the earth's relative position with the activities in this particular sphere of activity in the universe, it was chosen as the place for expression . . .

Then, as those expressed they were called the Sons of the Earth—or Sons of Man.

When the Creative Forces, God, made then the first man—or God-man—he was the beginning of the Sons of God.

Then those souls who entered through a channel made by God—not by thought, not by desire, not by lust, not by things that separated continually— were the Sons of God, the Daughters of God.

The Daughters of Men, then, were those who became the channels through which lust knew its activity; and it was in this manner then that the conditions were expressed as given of old, that the Sons of God looked upon the Daughters of Men and saw that they were fair, and LUSTED! (262–119)

Cayce found in the history of Atlantis the literal, or historical, basis for his interpretations of Genesis.*

The existence of Atlantis is still a highly speculative and controversial question, yet evidence mounts which supports the view that it once existed. Yet the readings make reference to a Lemurian civilization, which antedates Atlantis.* They also allude, rather obscurely, to civilizations called Da, Og, and Oz.

Although some remnants of this distant history can be found, it appears material science will never be able to definitely prove their existence. As the readings state, souls were not so closely knit in matter then, and thus these civilizations were more as "mental" or "thought-form" experiences.

The only records which remain exist on the ethers of Time and Space—the Akashic Record, the source from which Edgar Cayce drew all his information. This record can be read by anyone who, through spiritual development, achieves attunement to the universal forces.

Then through Mu, Oz, Atlantis—with the breaking up of these—why, WHY no records of these if there were the civilizations that are ordinarily accredited to them by the interpreting of the records made by entities or souls upon the skein of what? Time and Space!

But he only that has recognized Patience within self may indeed make the record as an experience in the consciousness of any. (262–115)

In a life reading, Cayce was able to trace back the origin of a young man's homosexual problem to a pre-Adamic experience. The entity then had manifested as an androgynous "thought-projection."

*For a detailed study of the entire Atlantean epoch, see Edgar Evans Cayce, *Edgar Cayce on Atlantis* (Paperback Library).

. . . we find the entity was in the Atlantean land and in those periods before Adam was in the earth. The entity was among those who were then "thought-projections," and the physical being had the union of sex in the one body, and yet [was] a real musician on pipes or reed instruments. (5056–1)

The following describes another pre-Adamic experience, and suggests the nature of the spiritual and mental climate prevailing.

. . . in the Atlantean land the entity was the time-keeper for those who were called things, or the servants, or the workers of the peoples, and the entity felt latent and manifest, as in the present, the wanting to reform, to change things, so that every individual soul had the right to freedom of speech, freedom of thought, freedom of activity.

For to the entity, even in those periods of man's unfoldment (for this was before Adam), the entity found during its activities the desire to improve, to make better those environs for the workers of that period. That alone brought into the entity's consciousness of man's position, the need of a pattern.

And the entity saw, the entity felt the need of God's hand in what evil, or Satan, had brought in the earth. (5249–1)

Although the events in Genesis took place amidst the thriving civilization of Atlantis when many of the characters and creatures of mythology inhabited the earth, the writers of Scripture are not concerned with the details of history. Their sole concern was centered on the Light of Genesis 1:3 and its manifestations in the earth.

Distortions and variations of the Light—such as giants, talking serpents, and later, the pagans—are acknowledged when necessary to the narrative, but never a sub-

ject by itself to be discussed, described, or otherwise
dwelt upon.

The writers were concerned with the perfection of
God. It is the Christ-Light and its development that is
followed throughout.

He, that Christ-consciousness, is that first spoken of
in the beginning when God said, "Let there be light,
and there was light." And that is the light manifested
in the Christ. First it became physically conscious
in Adam. And as in Adam we all die, so in the last
Adam—Jesus, becoming the Christ—we are all made
alive. (2879-1)

The Six Days of Creation

Although the "dark side" of Creation has been dwelt
upon in the preceding, it is necessary in order to establish an essential part of the Cayce philosophy—the conditions which made necessary the coming of Adam and the
later raising up of the nation Israel.

From the Beginning, souls were involved with materiality at all different levels, from the highest to the lowest,
from the lightest to the darkest.

Cayce is unique in his interpretation of the Six Days
of Creation as the evolving consciousness of those Sons of
God who were projecting into materiality and experiencing it through the Light.

The Six Days describes the manner in which God
directed the manifestation of His Spirit in materiality. It
is the evolution of those Images first formed in Spirit.

The first Day arose from the recognition of the Light
after a period of Darkness, or separation.

Do study creation, man's relationship to God. What is
light, that came into the earth, as described in the
3rd verse of Genesis 1? Find that light in self. It isn't

13

the light of the noonday sun, nor the moon, but rather of the Son of Man. (3491-1)

Time began through a consciousness of separation. In God's Mind there is no division. All is One.

"Let there be light," then, was that consciousness that Time began to be a factor in the experience of those creatures that had entangled themselves in matter; and became what we know as the influences in a material plane . . .

Hence, as we see, the divisions were given then for the day, the night; and then man knew that consciousness [which] made him aware that the morning and the evening were the first day. (262-115)

Or, as illustrated, the Day becomes the first day of the consciousness of separation from the forces [from] which the power, or the activity, is in action. . . .

Darkness, that it had separated—that a soul had separated itself from the light. Hence He called into being Light, and the awareness began. (262-56)

The Second Day reflects the consciousness which was caused by the division of Spirit. The earth, as it took form, divided into two great forces, Water and Earth —Mind and Matter!

More awareness is developed on the Third Day. An interesting concept is seen in the following:

Water, as manifest, [is] the *beginning* of life. Over large bodies of water, then, do many men of many lands learn that [which] is hard to be understood by those on land . . . Hence, many are given to dwell near large bodies of water, where sands and sea, where much comes that may not be touched by hands, may not be seen with the human eye, but is felt in the heart and trains the soul.

Wonders are often given as to why the restlessness of waves causes *quietness* from within. The answering of that from within self to the far call of the Spirit, of "God *moved* over the face of the waters and dry land appeared"; that man in his coming might make *manifest* the varied forms of the expression of *God* in his universe. (900–465)

As the earth began to move out of itself into its various manifestations, there came the awareness of the powers of reproduction, and the "seed within the seed." Genesis describes God's creations as "after its kind" and that He saw that "it was good." This distinguishes them from the selfish creations which were neither "good" nor "after its kind," which was the Spirit of God.

Each thought, as things, has its seed, and if planted, or when sown in one or another ground, brings its own fruit; for thoughts *are* things, and as their currents run must bring their own seed. (288–29)

The notes from Edgar Cayce's Bible class record these comments about the seed of Genesis and its significance.

"We can make a pattern of everything in nature, but we can't make it reproduce. We can't give it life. The seed of all vegetation is within the earth, because the power to reproduce was given to it by the Spirit from the beginning.

"The first principle was that God moved out of Himself. Consequently everything created has the seed within itself and creates by moving out of itself. Life in all its forms is God, and has the power within for its own reproduction."

On the Third Day, the spiritual force in natural elements is recognized.

Q-4 What *are* "the forces of the natural elements"?
A-4 Fire, earth, air, water. These are the *natural* elements in the physical plane, and—as the forces of these have the influence—as the *spirit* of the air . . . The *Spirit* of each! see? (288-27)

On the Fourth Day the Solar System was recognized as the source of particular forces and powers which could be used "for signs and for seasons."

In the beginning, as our own planet, earth, was set in motion, the placing of other planets began the ruling of the destiny of all matter as created, just as the division of waters was and is ruled by the moon in its path about the earth; just so in the higher creation, as it began, is ruled by the action of the planets about the earth.
The strongest power in the destiny of man is the sun, first; then the closer planets, or those that are coming into ascendancy at the time of the birth of the individual; but let it be understood here, no action of any planet or any of the phases of the sun, moon, or any of the heavenly bodies surpasses the rule of Man's individual will power—the power given by the Creator of man in the beginning, when he became a living soul, with the power of choosing for himself. (254-2)

For, remember, all of these planets, stars, universes, were made for the ENTITY and its associates to rule, and not to be ruled by them, save as an individual entity gives itself to their influence. (2830-2)

When the earth brought forth its Life—the creations of the animals, of sea, sky and land—we have the Fifth Awareness, or state of consciousness.

The Sixth Day brings forth the creation of Man, and the soul partook of both spiritual and physical awareness. The sixth state is the level of the god-man.

Two interpretations of Genesis 1:27 are possible, and both of them are correct. It is an indication of the birth of the soul. It is not part of the earth creation. The animal is the highest order of that evolution. Man is a separate creation in itself, and was first created in spirit.

The second view is that, because of the need for a perfect man, once the earth had evolved to its completeness, then the physical *pattern* for the body of man —or his soul—was imaged in God's Mind. Thus, Genesis 1:27 is a harbinger of the physical creation in Genesis 2.

. . . the preparation for the needs of man has gone down many, many thousands and millions of years, as is known in this plane, for the needs of man in the hundreds and thousands of years to come.

Man is man, and God's order of creation, which he represents even as His Son, who is the representative of the Father, took on the form of Man, the highest of the creation in the plane, and became to man that element that shows and would show, and will show the way, the directing way, the Life, the Water, the Vine, to the everlasting, when guided and kept in that manner . . . (3744-4)

When the earth evolved to the point where all the necessary elements were present for sustaining life in this form, we have the advent of Adam, and the coming of the Sons of God.

Man was made in the beginning, as the ruler over those elements as . . . prepared in the earth plane for his needs. When the plane became . . . such [that] man was capable of being sustained by the forces and conditions as were upon the face of the earth plane, man appeared not from that already created, but as the Lord over all that was created, and in man there is found that in the living man, all of that that may be found without in the whole, whole world or earth plane . . . the SOUL OF MAN is that making him above all animal, vegetable, mineral kingdoms of the earth plane. (3744–4)

And, remember, man, the soul of man, the body of man, the mind of man, is nearer to limitlessness than anything in creation. (281–55)

On the Seventh Day, God rested.

Sure, it is indicated that He rested on the 7th day— to take stock, or to let His purpose flow through that which had been made, that it might be perfected in itself. (3491–1)

The Seventh Plane could be considered as one of contemplation and review. All that which was destined for manifestation in the earth plane had been perfected within itself, in the Mind of God.

Now His Spirit flowed into these creations, giving them Life:

Q–3 Please explain the statement in Genesis, "In six days God made the heavens and the earth and rested the seventh day."

A–3 . . . When it is considered (as was later given, or *written* even before this was written) that "a thousand years is as but a day and a day as but a thousand years in the sight of the Lord," then it may be comprehended that this was colored by the writer in his desire to express to the people the power of the living God—rather than a statement of six days as man comprehends days in the present. Not that it was an impossibility—but rather that men under the environ should be impressed by the omnipotence of that they were called on to worship as God. (262–57)

Chapter 2
(Genesis 2)

The Coming of Adam

And all the trees of the field were not yet in the ground, and every herb of the field had not yet sprung up; for the Lord God had not yet caused it to rain upon the earth, and there was no man to till the ground. [Genesis 2:5; Lamsa trans.]

Chapter 2 begins with the actual manifestation in the earth of those spiritual images fashioned in chapter 1.

In Genesis 1, God divided (in His Mind) the waters, created the seas, imaged the trees, herbs, and fruit; yet Genesis 2 recounts, ". . . no plant of the field was yet in the earth . . . for the Lord God had not caused it to rain." Man was created spiritually in chapter 1 and given dominion over the earth, but in the second ". . . there was no man to till the ground."

Clearly, two different creations are recounted there.

The readings assure us that Creation is not yet finished. It is still unfolding, an ongoing process. Perhaps even today, all the things which God has intended for this plane have not yet "sprung up."

But a powerful spring gushed out of the earth, and watered all the face of the ground. [Genesis 2:6]

The above verse is also taken from the Lamsa translation. This rendering suggests a dynamism lacking in the

21

King James, Edgar Cayce's Bible, which reads, ". . . there went up a great mist from the earth."

A correlation between a passage in the Book of Job and several Edgar Cayce Life Readings reveals a great hidden meaning in this 6th verse.

Water is symbolic of the source of Life in the earth, and is the first materialization of spirit.

As is known of all, water is a necessary element in the material forces for the sustaining of life in the material plane; hence this element is often called the mother of creation. *How* does water, then, supply that which nourishes in this material plane? Being made up of elements in itself that are the essence of that which may truly be called spiritual in itself, it gives that association or connection between the spiritual forces acting in the material elements of the earth, or material forces; hence in entering in the kingdom of the Father is knowing and following and *being* those elements that supply the needs of that which builds in the material plane towards the continuity of the spiritual forces manifest in the earth. So one enters, then, through that Door with the Savior, that brings that necessary force in the life of others, and in saving others saves self. How came the Son of man the Way that leads to perfection in heaven and in earth? In overcoming the forces in nature and in earth, by giving of self for others; hence becoming the Savior of others becomes the Son and one with the Father. (262–28)

The "powerful spring" suggests a definite and dynamic action of the Spirit; because of its textual relationship, it is also interconnected with the coming of Adam.

But what action is being symbolized here?

In Job 38 (reading 262–55 states Job was written by Melchizedek, one of the early incarnations of soul who later incarnated as Jesus), the Lord, speaking to

Job, states "the foundations of the earth were laid" when "the morning stars sang together, and all the Sons of God shouted for joy."

In the Life Readings, Cayce was able to trace for several individuals an initial experience with the earth which dated from this period "When the Sons of God came together," and is the same event described symbolically as "a powerful spring gushing from the earth."

... in the beginning, when all forces were given in the spiritual force, and the morning stars sang together in the glory of the coming of the Lord and the God to make the giving of man's influence and [the] developing in the world's forces [this entity was there]. (2497-1)

... when the earth's forces were called into existence, and the Sons of God came together, and the sounding of the coming of the Man was given, .. this entity was there. (234-1)

This was the dynamic action of the Spirit!

[This entity was] In the beginning, when the first of the elements were given, and the forces set in motion that brought about the sphere . . . called [the] earth plane, and when the morning stars sang together, and the whispering winds brought the news of the coming of man's indwelling, of the spirit of the Creator, and he, man, became the living soul. The entity came into being with this multitude. (294-8)

Two individuals were told they had been spiritual messengers of this cosmic event.

... in the days when the Sons of God came together to reason in the elements as to the appearance of man

23

in physical on earth's plane . . . this entity was among those chosen as the messenger to all the realm. (137–4)

. . . the entity was in the beginning, when the Sons of God came together to announce to Matter a way being opened for the souls of men, the souls of God's creation, to come again to the awareness of their error.

The entity then . . was among those ANNOUNC-ING same. (2156–2)

The origin of the "chosen people" began with entities such as the following who chose to make "heaven's forces" manifest through "the creature called man."

When the forces of the universe came together, upon the waters was the coming together of the Sons of God. The morning stars sang together. Over the face of the waters was the voice of the glory of the coming of the plane for man's indwelling.

When the earth in its form became a place, and afterward able to be an abode for the creature called man, this entity chose that through this manner, it, that entity, that part of the whole—would—would—through these creatures—make manifest heaven and heaven's forces through these elements. (341–1)

The coming together of the Sons of God created an impression on one soul which has sustained it through the eons that followed.

. . . when the Sons of God came together to announce the coming of man's dwelling on the earth plane. This then . . . has ever been the indwelling force through-out the ages . . . of the love of the Creator. (2553–8)

A close associate of Edgar Cayce's was told in his reading:

. . . when souls sought or found manifestation in materiality by the projection of themselves into matter—as became thought forms—and when this had so enticed the companions or souls of the Creator, first we had then the creation in which "God breathed into man [God-made] the breath of life and he became a living soul," with the abilities to become godlike.

Hence we find the first preparation or estate, or manner in which those souls might through material manifestations acclaim—by the living, by the being—that which was and is and ever will be consistent with the purposes of creation—was given into the estate of man.

The entity was among those first who through those channels came into consciousness awareness of the relationships of the material man to the Creative Forces; that came into material activity during the early portions of man's CONSCIOUSNESS of being an independent entity, or body, in a material existence. (257–20)

Adam and his descendants represent those who entered in the earth through the Mind of the Maker, or in accordance with the pattern outlined in Genesis 1.

The earth and the universe, as related to man, came into being through the Mind—Mind—of the Maker, and, as such, has its same being much as each atomic force multiplies in itself, or as worlds are seen and being made in the present period, and as same became (earth, we are speaking of) an abode for man, man entered as man, through the Mind of the Maker, see? in the form of flesh man; that which carnally might die, decay, become dust, entering into material conditions. The Spirit, the gift of God, that man might be One with Him, with the concept of man's creative forces throughout the physical world. (900–227)

Cayce constantly reiterates, "Mind is the Builder." The Sons of God, as they entered the earth, were attuned, influenced, animated by the spiritual mind of the Creator.

For, was not the physical being made from all else that grew? For, of the dust of the earth was the body-physical created. But the *Word,* the MIND, is the controlling factor of its shape, its activity, from the source, the spiritual—the spiritual entity.

Thus there are within the abilities of each soul that ability to choose that as will keep the body, the mind, the portion of the spirit, attuned to holiness—or oneness with Him. (263–13)

Those who entered with this awareness found in themselves that ability to "subdue the earth."

. . . "*Subdue* the earth." For all therein has been given for man's purpose, for man's convenience, for man's understanding, for man's interpreting of God's relationship to man. And when man makes same only a gratifying, a satisfying of self, whether in appetite, in desire, in self motives for self-aggrandizement, self-exaltation, these become—as from old—stumbling blocks. But he that hath put off the old and put on the new is regenerated in the new Adam, and last Adam, in the Christ.

And as many as have done so may find in themselves that knowledge of His presence abiding with them; so that things, conditions, circumstances, environs, no longer become stumbling blocks—rather have they become stepping stones for the greater view wherein they each may gain at least in part first, gradually growing in grace, in the understanding to know those glories, those beauties God hath prepared for them that know the way of the Cross *with* the Christ as the Good Shepherd. (262–99)

Those souls who entered with the Light entered in harmony with the natural elements of this plane.

And, as was given, be thou wise—not in thine own conceit, but in the wisdom of the Lord, and *subdue* the earth: or *making* these . . . coordinant with that which is in thine own body, mind, and soul.

For, when the earth was brought into existence or into time and space, all the elements that are *without* man may be found in the *living* human body.

Hence these in coordination, as we see in nature, as we see in the air, as we see in the fire or in the earth, make the soul, body, and mind *one* coordinating factor with the universal creative energy we call God. (557-3)

Adam

In Genesis 1, God said, "Let us make man"—creation by Divine Fiat, or through the Word. In Genesis 2, God "formed" Adam* (or "man," as in the King James and New American Catholic translations). The suggestion here is a manipulation of materials and an action in Time.

Most liberal interpreters agree "man" and "Adam" carry the same meaning, indicating the origin of mankind, and not an individual. Yet the Cayce readings show that both a literal and symbolic meaning apply. Adam represents a race,† but is also an experience of one

---

*Lamsa translation.

†Unlike archeologists and other scholars who look for a physical race identified through blood lines, bone structure, and other physical features, the Adamic race which Cayce describes is one of Spirit whose members are identified by a common mode of thought and action.

. . . who is Israel? . . . Israel is the seeker after Truth. Who may this be? Those who put and hold trust in the fact that

soul—the first Adam, who, through his incarnations in the earth, became the Savior of man, the last Adam—Jesus who became the Christ.

When there was in the beginning a man's advent into the plane known as earth, and it became a living soul, amenable to the laws that govern the plane itself as presented, the Son of man entered the earth as the first man. Hence, the Son of Man, the Son of God, the Son of the First Cause, making manifest in a material body.

This was not the first spiritual influence, spiritual body, spiritual manifestation in the earth, but the first man—flesh and blood; the first carnal house, the first amenable body to the laws of the plane in its position in the universe. (5749-3)

After man was formed, God "breathed into his nostrils the breath of life; and man became a living soul." This is similar to the seventh day of creation when, the images being formed, God rested and allowed His spirit to flow into the pattern, animating His creation.

The following suggests new insights into this verse.

Q-4 Please explain, "He breathed on them, and saith unto them, Receive ye the Holy Ghost." (John 20:22)
A-4 . . . As the breath of life was breathed into the body of the man, see, so breathed He that of love and hope into the experience of those who were to become witnesses of Him in the material world.

---

they, as individuals, are children of the universal consciousness or God! (5377-1)
. . . the greater meaning of the word—Israel those called of God for a service before the fellowman. (587-6)
For those who seek are indeed Israel, and Israel indeed is ALL who seek; meaning not those as of the children of Abraham alone, but of every nation, every tribe, every tongue—Israel of the Lord! That is the full meaning of Israel. (2772-1)

Q-5 Does this verse have reference to the beginning as Adam?
A-5 In the same manner of beginning, yes. (5749-10)

. . . as the breath, the ether from the forces [that] come into the body of the human when born breathes the breath of life, as it becomes a living soul, provided it has reached that developing in the creation where the soul many enter and find the lodging place (3744-4)

The following suggests a state of cosmic consciousness.

Q-6 [Explain] the Holy Breath?
A-6 . . . As we say, the All-Seeing Eye of God, the All-Seeing Eye of self can only be attained when in attune to God. And when attuned, he hath breathed the Holy Breath on the activity of the entity. (2533-8)

The place of manifestation for this new race, and the individual soul of Adam, was in "a garden eastward in Eden."

"Eastward" is the direction of the sun. Thus the location of the garden symbolizes a condition close to the source of all life. Both Man and the Garden were projections of the God-consciousness.

"Eden" is not important as a place, but as a condition, an expression of consciousness by souls in the earth. It was the material experience of many and a record of it has been left in all parts of the world.

And out of the ground the Lord God made to grow every tree that is pleasant to the sight and good for food; and the Tree of Life also in the midst of the Garden, and the Tree of Knowledge of Good and Evil. (Genesis 2:9)

The Garden is a literal truth, an actual state and condition of the world at one time, but is also symbolic of man's body. Later the body is referred to as "the Temple" by teachers such as Jeremiah, Paul, and John. Jesus referred to his own body as "The Temple." (John 2:21) But in the beginning it is called "the Garden."

The existence of the Tree of Knowledge indicates the probability from the beginning of the perfect man's separation from the Source. The Father-God was aware of the possibility, yet did not know if, how, or when it would happen until the soul, by its own choice, caused it to be so.

We recall at this point that Joshua was aiding Moses in the composition and interpretation of this myth.

The two Trees are reflected in the two principles he later voiced in his great statement, so often quoted in the readings:

> *There is set before you good and evil, life and death, choose thou this day whom you will serve. As for me and my house, we will serve the Living God. (Joshua 24:15)*

These two principles of spirit still exist, as they did in the beginning. A soul can choose consistently to eat from the Tree of Life, and thus maintain his connection to the Source; or use his existence to experience the things of the world in a manner which gives him knowledge, yet results in separation and eventual death of the Spirit within.

"Death does not come in a moment, or even in an epoch, but if the soul continues to sin, continues 'to eat,' then it reaps its karma from the laws of cause and effect."

It was six hundred years before Adam died.

And again He has said, as He showed the way, as He fulfilled in giving His life, "In the day ye eat thereof ye shall surely die." Yet the tempter said, "Not surely die," for it may be put off; and it was—six hundred years—and yet death came, the pangs of the loss of self. (3188-1)

A Soul Group

And a river went out of Eden to water the garden, and from thence it was parted, and became four heads. (Genesis 2:10)

In verse 10 we again return to a water symbol—the river with four heads. Rivers in the natural world have one head and part into tributaries. Thus, this river is unlike any in the earth, and must be symbolic of a spiritual influence entering the earth. This river is the same as the "powerful spring" of verse 6.

Adam was a god-man, the first to enter the earth at-one with, or through, the Light. He entered as a living soul, manifesting the spiritual image in Genesis 1.

The readings declare that Adam (the soul who later became Jesus) did not enter alone. Many of the Sons of God who "shouted for joy" when the morning stars sang together came with him. 144,000 is the symbolic number—which may even be literal as well—of those who participated in this movement.

This influx is what is really meant and symbolized by the four-headed river.

When the earth brought forth the seed in her season, and man came in the earth plane as the lord of that in that sphere, man appeared in five places then at once—the five senses, the five reasons, the five spheres, the five developments, the five nations. (5748-1)

Man, in Adam (as a group; not as an individual), entered into the world (for he entered in five places at once, we see—called Adam in one, see?) . . . (900–227)

The following again calls to mind the existence of the "dark side" of creation and speaks of the decision made by the soul we know as Jesus, who became the Christ.

Then, as the sons of God came together and saw in the earth the unspeakable conditions becoming more and more for the self-indulgence, self-glorification, the ability to procreate through the very forces of their activity, we find that our Lord, our Brother CHOSE to measure up, to earn, to ATTAIN that companionship for man with the Father through the overcoming of SELF in the physical plane. (262–115)

Q–6 What is the explanation of "The Lamb slain *before* the foundation of the world?" (Revelation 13:8)
A–6 . . . As the Master gave, 'Before Abraham was, I AM—before the worlds were I AM." Hence, when there came the necessity in the realm of the spiritual home for the coming of the Lamb into the earth for its redemption, the Truth, the Light, the Offering was made. Hence the expression as given . . . Then, when we comprehend we realize there is no time, no space, and that the divinity of the man Jesus was perfect in his *own* activity in the earth. For, it was offered even from the first. (262–57)

Adam, who later became Jesus, manifested in the Atlantean environment.
The other points of entry are listed in the following.

Q–5 Was Atlantis one of the five points at which man appeared in the beginning, being the home of the red race?

A-5 One of the five points. As has been given, in what is known as Gobi, India, Carpathia, or in that known as the Andes, and [what is] known as in the western plain of what is now called America—the five places.

In their presentation, as we find, these—in the five places, as *man*. (Let's get the difference in that as first appeared [as thought-forms] in what is known as Atlantis, and that as *man* appearing from those projections in the five places—and, as has been given, from their environ took on that as became necessary for the meeting of those varying conditions under which their individualities and personalities began to put on form)—one in the white, another in the brown, another in the black, another in the red. (364-9)

This simultaneous projection is the explanation offered by Cayce as to why similar Creation myths and legends of the Fall are found in all parts of the world—it was all happening at the same time!

Q-6 The center or beginning of these projections was in Atlantis?
A-6 Was in Atlantis. Hence we have, as from the second incarnation there—or the story as is given in Judaism doesn't vary a great deal from that of the Chaldean; neither does it vary at all from that [which] *will* be discovered in Yucatan; nor does it vary a great deal from that as from the *older* ones of the Indian (East Indian, of course—as it is from the present). (364-9)

A later reading in this 364 series asked this pointed question.

Q-4 Why was the number five selected for the projection of the five races?

A–4 This, as we find, is that element which represents man in his physical form, and the attributes to which he may become conscious *from* the elemental or spiritual to the physical consciousness. As the senses; as the sensing *of* the various forces that bring to man the activities in the sphere in which he finds himself.

Q–5 Did the appearance of what became the five races occur simultaneously?

A–5 Occurred at once. (364–13)

The course of the five rivers is outlined and the lands they water are described. This description is included, not to pinpoint a definite location, but to make it all-inclusive. The Spirit was moving as one big stream of consciousness, manifesting in every possible way as part of man's new abode.

The river Pishon circled the land of Havilah, "where there is gold." (Genesis 2:11) Gold is one of the basic forces within man that produces or allows consciousness. Gold is the connecting link between mind and body. The presence of gold helps make this symbolic picture all-inclusive.

There are elements in the earth from which, to which, every atom of the body responds. Here we find that silver and gold are those necessary elements that are needed in body when mind has been attuned to Creative Forces for helpful influences. (3491–1)

The following is a description given by Cayce of the earth's surface at the time of the five projections.

In the first, or that known as the beginning, or in the Caucasian and Carpathian, or the Garden of Eden, in that land which lies now much in the desert, yet much in mountain and much in the rolling lands there. The extreme northern portions were then the

34

southern portions, or the polar regions were then turned to where they occupied more of the tropical and semi-tropical regions; hence it would be hard to discern or disseminate the change. The Nile entered into the Atlantic Ocean. What is now the Sahara was an inhabited land and very fertile. What is now the central portion of this country, or the Mississippi basin, was then all in the ocean; only the plateau was existent, or the regions that are now portions of Nevada, Utah, and Arizona formed the greater part of what we know as the United States. That along the Atlantic board formed the outer portion then, or the lowlands of Atlantis. The Andean, or the Pacific coast of South America, occupied then the extreme western portion of Lemuria. The Urals and the northern regions of same were turned into a tropical land. The desert in the Mongolian land was then the fertile portion . . . The oceans were then turned about; they no longer bear their names, yet from whence obtained they their names? What is the legend, even as to their names? (364-13)

From a Life Reading, we find another indication of this projection.

. . . we find the entity was in the Egyptian land, the Indian land, the lands from which most of those came for one of the branches of the first appearances of the Adamic influence that came as five at once into the expressions in the earth, or the expression in that now known as the Gobi land. (1210-1)

There were also other centers that were developing. For in the projections they began as many, and in creating influences they began as five—or in those centers where crystallization or projection had taken on such form as to become what was called man. (877-26)

35

The soul whom we know as Adam, and later as Jesus, we know by other names through his subsequent incarnations in the earth. His Old Testament lives include those as Melchizedek, Enoch, Joseph, Joshua, and Jeshua. The readings state *before* this soul had an earthly name, his name as a soul, or celestial being, was *Amilius*.

These [the Sons of God] were all together [in spirit] in Amilius. They were material bodies as came in Adam. (288–29)

And the Lord God took the man, and put him into the garden of Eden to dress it and to keep it.

And the Lord God commanded the man, saying, Of every Tree of the garden thou mayest freely eat:

But of the Tree of Knowledge of Good and Evil, thou shalt not eat of it; for in the day thou eatest thereof thou shalt surely die. (Genesis 2:15–17)

In the 9th verse, the existence of the Tree of the Knowledge of Good and Evil was acknowledged; in the 17th verse, as the Sons of God enter into the earth, they are told definitely what their relationship to this "Tree" should be.

Failure to heed the warning will result in the same loss of understanding and awareness as the spiritual darkness which preceded the creation of the earth.

For that purpose came He into the earth . . . that there might be completed that as He had given, "In the day ye eat thereof, ye shall surely die." In the day thou sinnest, ye have destroyed, then, that something in thine consciousness that must be paid, that must be met in thyself. (3028–1)

And out of the ground the Lord God formed every beast of the field; and every fowl of the air; and brought them unto Adam to see what he would call them. (Genesis 2:19)

According to a Cayce reading, this verse contains a hidden meaning.

Hence, it is given in thy writings of Scripture (although in a hidden manner, ye may observe if ye will look) how Adam named those that were brought before him in creation. Their NAME indicates to the carnal mind their relationships in the sex condition or question. (5747-3)

The desire for companionship is innate in God, and was the first cause for the creation of souls. Souls, created in the Image of God, carried the same desire.

The story, the tale (if chosen to be called such) is one and the same. The apple, as "the apple of the eye," the desire of that companionship innate in that created, as innate in the Creator, *that* brought companionship into creation itself. Get that one! (364-5)

With the evolution of the animal kingdom, souls began using various phases of animal life as the negative force for their projections. At first this had occurred spiritually, through the creation of thought-forms. Eventually, as these thoughts became more crystallized and hardened through the living power which had been projected into them, they became living creatures and began to populate the earth—a mixture of thought forms and animal life. Great monstrosities evolved, and many other sordid and unnatural creatures which were eventually eliminated at the time of the Flood.

It is interesting to note that verse 19 of the King James translation, when the animals are brought before him, is the first reference to Adam by name. Until then he is referred to solely as "the man." The Lamsa translation refers to Adam throughout. The Catholic New American Bible uses "the man" exclusively.

Liberal theologians claim Genesis is a symbolic account of the evolutionary events in the history of mankind, created from speculations of early man once consciousness had evolved. "The man," or "Adam," is the personification of the entire human family. Some say Moses was aware of other forms of human life, but that he represented the highest order, the most advanced, and his account is not about mankind in general, but only of his race, or superior order. The Humanist scholars assert man evolved from the lower forms of life, and was not "created."

The Fundamentalists assert literally man was a spontaneous creation of God, and did not evolve. They also claim that man is literally descended from two original parents, Adam and Eve.

According to the Cayce readings, a great deal of Truth is found in both positions, but neither one has "all the truth." There is evolution, and man's physical frame was modeled after the highest of the primates—the great ape. The ape was used as a pattern. But the soul, with its consciousness and creativity, improved even upon that form. Thus man *appeared*. There was a set of first parents, a literal Adam and Eve. But they are also symbolic of all the "first parents" in all the five lines of the Adamic race, and were the highest order of the many varied forms of soul-life that were manifesting.

Adam's search for a helper, or "helpmeet," suggests a larger pattern. The Life Readings show that many Sons of God came in with Amilius (or Adam) as helpers. One woman asked in her reading:

Q–1 In Atlantis, was I associated with Amilius? If so, how?
A–1 One as projected by that entity as to a ruler or *guide* for many, with its associating entity. (288–29)

38

Many of the "trapped" souls had hooves, scales, fins, etc., as portions of their material bodies.

One of Cayce's Bible class students was told in her reading:

This entity was the companion of that beginning of activity in the Atlantean land. Thus, not as a mother of creation . . . but as an advisor to those who would change in their form of activities; or the attempts as later expressed in the entity of being rid of the appendages of materiality. (2454-3)

This was the beginning of the effort to get souls to disengage from animal associations.

The land was among those in which there was the first appearance of those that were as separate entities or souls disentangling themselves from material or that we know as animal associations. For the projections of these had come from those influences that were termed Lemure, or Lemurian, or the land of Mu.

These then we find as the period when there was the choice of that soul that became in its final earthly experience the Savior, the Son in the earth dwellings, or of those as man sees or comprehends as the children of men. (877-10)

Perhaps in verse 19, when the King James changes the general term "the man" to the specific "Adam," we have a switch in focus from the collective and representational race experience to the specific, singular, and unique experience of Adam, the soul who later became Jesus. Amilius (or Adam) was the leader of this whole movement and it was through his choice that the sex issue or question was settled.

The question before Adam was how he could produce or propagate one of his own kind, or species, in the earth.

Instead of turning to the animal kingdom, Adam drew upon the spiritual resources within himself for the propagation of his "helpmeet."

> And the Lord God caused a deep sleep to fall upon Adam and he slept; and he took one of his ribs . . . and the rib, which the Lord God had taken from man, made he a woman, and brought her unto the man. (Genesis 2:21)

The "deep sleep" indicates a state of meditation.

These are, as seen, the records made by the man on the mount [Moses], that this Amilius—Adam, as given —first discerned that from himself, not of the beasts about him, could be drawn—*was* drawn—that which made for the propagation *of* beings *in* the flesh, that made for that companionship as seen by creation in the material worlds about same. (364–5)

Adam, we remember, was "a living soul." He was not encased in the dense, flesh frame of man today.

Yea, but the individual of that period was not so closely knit in matter. (281–42)

As a body of "light" or energy, he was able to control its shape by the nature of his thought.

As to their forms in the physical sense, these were rather of the nature of thought-forms, or able to push out of themselves in that direction in which [their] development took shape. . . ." (364–3)

All souls were created in the beginning as both male and female; or, more accurately, *neither* male nor female as we understand the terms today. The soul itself has no sex, but has both positive and negative energies. As it comes into materiality, it takes on either the positive or negative pattern, according to its development and the purpose to be accomplished.

The time came when Adam (as a race) had to be divided into positive and negative forces. This division was necessary in order for the Adamic race to propagate perfect physical bodies through which the entrapped or "lost" souls could manifest and gradually find their way back to the Source. This form of reproduction had to be accomplished through kindred beings—souls—and not the animal kingdom.

Thus, when the deep sleep fell on Adam (the individual), he took on the active, positive, male force.

". . . He breathed into him the breath of Life and he became a living soul." As the sleep fell upon him, and the soul separated—through the taking of man's portion—and He becoming a portion of man. (282-3)

. . . then—from out of the self—was brought that as was to be the helpmeet, *not* just [the] companion of the body. (364-7)

Eve was created to complete and complement Adam's positive or male expression.

How received woman her awareness? Through the sleep of the man! Hence *intuition* is an attribute of that made aware through the suppression of those forces from that from which it sprang, yet endowed *with* all of those abilities and forces of its Maker. (5754-2)

This does not mean Adam split or divided his soul, nor that Eve was an inferior creation. Both were complete entities, entire souls, and, as the above indicates, were "endowed with all those abilities and forces of [their] Maker."

Adam was able to project out of his own body the negative substance through which another soul, by suppressing its positive, could manifest.

Perhaps the closest analogy we have to the creation of Eve from the body of Adam is in the claim made by spiritualist mediums who are able to produce disincarnate spirits at their seances. This materialization is done, the medium states, from an ectoplasmic substance which he is able to project from his body while in a meditative state. The discarnate moves into the ectoplasmic field and molds it according to his own features, to be recognizable to those at the seance.

The creation of the body of Eve, drawn from self and not the animal kingdom, was a spiritual procreation, an immaculate form of conception. The indication is that the descendants of Adam were practicing this manner of propagation up to the time of Noah and the Flood. After Noah, the knowledge was generally lost, but restored (or brought to mind again) through the Virgin Birth.

> Were this turned to that period when this desire, then becomes consecrated . . . again in the virgin body of the mother of the Son of man, we see . . . that even that of the flesh may be—with the proper concept, [the] proper desire in all its purity—consecrated to the *living* forces as manifest by the ability in that body so brought into being, as to make a way of escape for the *erring* man. (364-6)

Uniting the opposing forces, the positive and negative, male and female, and bringing them into a creative balance and stabilizing our relationships with our "opposites," becomes the way of returning and reuniting with the Oneness of Spirit.

Q–6 Is the destiny of woman's body to return to the

rib of man, out of which it was created? If so, how; and what is "the rib"?

A–6 With this ye touch upon delicate subjects, upon which *much* might be said respecting the necessity of that *union* of influences or forces that are divided in the earth in sex, in which all must become what? As He gave in answer to the question, "Whose wife will she be?"

In the heavenly kingdom ye are neither married nor given in marriage; neither is there any such thing as sex; ye become as *one*—in the union of that from which, *of* which, ye have been the portion from the beginning. (262–86)

Chapter 3
(Genesis 3)

The Fall of Man

. . . we see the creation of the world, as the awareness of these influences that have become enmeshed, entangled into matter; that they are seeking they know not what.

For that desire to procreate in self, or to hold to selfish interests, has grown—grown—until it IS—what did He give?—*the prince of this world, the prince of this world!*

Know that He who came as our director, as our brother, as our Savior, has said that the prince of this world has no part in Him, nor with Him. (John 14: 30)

Then as we become more and more aware within ourselves of the answering of the experiences, we become aware of what He gave to those that were the first of *God's* projection—not man but God's projection into the earth, Adam and Eve.

And then in their early day they were tempted by the prince of this world, and partook of same. (262-115)

The readings are very definite about the cause of Adam's Fall. Sin came into God's Creation through the misuse of the God-Force at the sexual level. This was the real temptation, the "forbidden fruit" offered to Eve.

The apple, then, that desire for that which made for the associations that bring carnal-minded influences of that brought as sex influence, know in a material world, and the partaking of same is that which brought the influence in the lives of that in the symbol of the serpent, that made for that which creates the desire that may be only satisfied in gratification of carnal forces, as partake of the world and its influences about same—rather than of the spiritual emanations from which it has its source.

Will control—inability of will control, if we may put it in common parlance.* (364-5)

Perhaps the Serpent made Eve aware of that mysterious substance which was now the home for her soul —her own body, undefiled and unexplored.

And when the woman saw that the tree was good for food, and that it was pleasant to the eyes, and a tree to be desired to make one wise, she took of the fruit thereof, and did eat, and gave also unto her husband with her; and he did eat. (Genesis 3:6)

Cayce's thoughts on Conception and Childbirth are worth noting here.

The readings placed great emphasis on the ideals and purposes of the parents toward sexual union, conception, and childbirth. Their mental and spiritual ideals can exert a more powerful influence on the unborn child than the physical forces of heredity and environment. A long series of readings, part of the 281 series

*Although the symbol of the serpent covers all activities which keep souls out of attunement with God, the present interpretation will center on its manifestation as carnal desire.
This is not the only interpretation, but one that is practical and applicable. Of course "carnal desire", as spoken of in the reading, is not limited to sexual lusts, but with all activities that use spiritual energies for gratifying of material urges.

devoted to the book of The Revelation, investigated such desire . . . is phenomena extensively.

The conclusion of this series is succinctly stated in the following.

Q–6 It is the spiritual activity within the body of the parents, or the lack of it, that determines the influence predominant in the life of their child.
A–6 This is true. (281–54)

There are many examples in Scripture—and they will be commented upon throughout—where the spiritual preparation of the parents resulted in the birth of children who became the great leaders and examples for Israel.

The neglect of these activities produced Israel's great sinners and stumbling blocks And the first example of this is Cain.

Eula Allen, in her *Creation Trilogy*,* suggests that Cain was actually fathered by a Serpent-being who seduced Eve.

Literally, the serpent could have been a crystallized thought-form of a soul. Eve could easily have been beguiled into listening to this handsome being who was already wise in the ways of the world, and knew exactly how to present himself to her.

The following thoughts are taken from the Edgar Cayce Bible class notes.

"No doubt that one who tempted Eve presented himself in a very beautiful and desirable way, so that Eve believed him and forgot, for the moment, God's commandment which, apparently, she had received second-hand from Adam. The serpent (so-called) seemed much more real to her.

*(Virginia Beach, Va.: A.R.E. Press). An extensive and thorough study of Genesis and Creation.

It's the same today. Unless we constantly seek guidance from within, we are apt to be led into temptation by the things of this world"

Was Cain propagated through the serpent—or fathered through the self-indulgence of our first parents? In either case, Cain is clearly the result of The Fall, the first creation of the created.

The serpent is the earthly form (and first manifestation of evil mentioned in Scripture) of that spirit which rebelled in Heaven, still working to undermine God's plan for reuniting His children with Him. Adam and Eve, until they fell, were one with the consciousness of God.

It was the eating, the partaking, of knowledge; knowledge without wisdom, or that as might bring pleasure, satisfaction, gratifying . . . Thus in the three-dimensional phases of consciousness such manifestations become as pleasing to the eye, pleasant to the body appetites. Thus the interpretation of the experience, or of that first awareness of deviation from the divine law, is given in the form as of eating of the Tree of Knowledge.

Who, what influence, caused this, ye ask?

It was that influence which had, or would, set itself in opposition to the souls remaining, or the entity remaining, in that state of at-onement (815-7)

A Pattern for All

The Fall in Eden symbolizes the experiences of the twin-souls Adam and Eve, yet it also represents the pattern for all the Sons of God who entered with them.

Man, in Adam (as a group, not as an individual) entered into the world (for he entered in five places at once, we see—called Adam in one, see?) and as man's concept [came] to that point wherein man walked not after the ways of the Spirit but after the desires of the flesh, *sin* entered—that is, away from the Face of the Maker, see? and death then became man's portion, *spiritually*, see? for the physical death existed from the beginning; for to create one must die . . . (900–227)

This universal pattern is reflected in this Life Reading which describes a temptation similar to Eve's.

. . . the entity was in the Atlantean land, during those periods of the early rise in the land of the sons of Belial as oppositions, that became more and more materialized as the powers were applied for self-aggrandizement.

The entity was among the children of the Law of One that succumbed to the wiles—and it may be WELL interpreted in that answer recorded in Holy Writ—"Ye shall not *surely* die, but it is pleasant for the moment, and for the satisfying of longings within."

Thus did the entity begin to use spiritual forces for the satisfying of material appetites. (2850–1)

And the eyes of them were opened, and they knew that they were naked . . . And they heard the voice of the Lord God walking in the garden in the cool of the day; and Adam and his wife hid themselves from the presence of the Lord God amongst the trees of the garden. (Genesis 3:7–8)

Both Adam and Eve became self-conscious, aware that the appetites of their bodies were at variance with the desires of the spirit.

The new consciousness brought fear.

. . . with these changes coming in the experience of . . . Adam and Eve, the knowledge of their position, or that as is known in the material world today as desires and physical bodily charms, the understanding of sex, sex relationships, came into the experience. With these

49

came the natural fear of that as had been forbidden, that they know themselves to be a part of but not *of* that as partook of [the] earthly, or the desires in the manner [of those] as were *about* them, in that as had been their heritage. (364-6)

Apparently, the temptation and Fall were part of the Divine Plan, a necessary experience which had been foreseen by Amilius while in the spiritual state.

. . . as the first begotten of the Father, [who] came as Amilius in the Atlantean land and allowed himself to be led in ways of selfishness. (364-8)

The Fall also involved a clairvoyant experience for Adam.

Q-19 When did the knowledge come to Jesus that He was to be the savior of the world?
A-19 When He fell in Eden. (2067-7)

The God-Force became sexual force, or carnal force, in the Garden. The destiny of Adam, after the Fall, was to restore and demonstrate the full potential of man's creative energies in the flesh. This was realized through the Immaculate Conception of Mary (who had been Eve) and in the life of Jesus through his ministry and especially his Resurrection, the ultimate triumph over the physical.

This reading was devoted solely to the sex question.

Yes, we have the question here regarding sex and sex relationships . . . This has been the problem throughout man's experience or man's sojourn in the earth; since taking bodily form with the attributes of the animal in which he had *projected* himself as a portion of, that he might through the self gain that activity which was visualized to him in those relationships in the earth.

Hence slow has been the progress through the ages. And as has been seen, and as may be gained by a study of man's development, this . . . has ever been a problem before man.

This is ever, and will ever be, a question, a problem, until there is the greater spiritual awakening within man's experience that this phase biologically, sociologically, or even from the analogical experience, must be as a stepping stone for the greater awakening; and as the exercising of an influence in man's experience in the Creative Forces for the reproduction of species, rather than for the satisfying or gratifying of a biological urge within the individual that partakes or has partaken of the first causes of man's encasement in body in the earth. (5747-3)

The different natures of Cain and Abel may reflect a change in Adam and Eve concerning the purposes for sexual union. Cain was rebellious, self-indulgent, and unruly. Abel sought the approval of his Creator.

Seth, the third son, is the beginning of a nation dedicated to God and to the proper uses of the creative energies which Man had been given.

Train him, train her, train *them* rather in the sacredness of that which has come to them as a privilege, which has come to them as a heritage, from a falling away, to be sure; but through the purifying of the body in thought, in act, in certainty, it may make for a people, a state, a nation that may indeed herald the coming of the Lord. (5747-3)

The First Adam and the Last Adam

For ALL that ever was and ever is to be learned is [that] "The Lord thy God is one"—ONE . . . No matter in what clime, under what name, all must come to that as was from the beginning. For, know that He—who

51

was lifted up on the Cross in Calvary—was . . . also he that first walked among men at the beginning of man's advent into flesh! For He indeed was and is the first Adam, the last Adam; that is the way, the truth, the light! (2402-2)

Q-5 What was meant by "As in the first Adam, sin entered, so in the last Adam all shall be made alive"?

A-5 Adam's entry into the world in the beginning, then must become the savior of the world, as it was committed to his care. "Be thou fruitful, multiply, and *subdue* the earth!" Hence . . . Adam, the first Adam, the last Adam, became—then—that that is *given* the *power over* the earth, and—as in each soul the first to be conquered is self—then *all things*, conditions and elements, are subject unto that self! (364-7)

The story of the Old Testament is one of evolution—spiritual, mental, and physical. The growth in attitude from the self-centeredness in the first Adam to the spiritual directions of the Last is demonstrated in the following:

Let's draw comparisons of man made perfect through experience, and man WILLFULLY being disobedient.

In the first, we find man listening to those influences which were at variance to God's way. Then in the temple, even at twelve, we find the perfect man seeking, asking, and answering as to man's relationship to God. . . .

Draw the comparison within thyself as to those experiences indicated in the 1st, 2nd, and 3rd of Genesis and those in the 2nd of Luke—where we find our pattern, our lesson . . . one willfully seeking to know the relationship to the Creator, or the answer, "Know ye not that I must be about my Father's business?" How different from that other, "The *woman* thou gavest me, SHE persuaded me, and I did eat!" (262-125)

The following indicates a similar evolution in Eve, who listened, but did not weigh the words of Satan or their implications.

. . . seek not for knowledge alone. For, look—LOOK—what it brought EVE. Look rather for that wisdom which was eventually founded in she that was addressed as the handmaid of the Lord, and who "pondered those things in her heart," as to how and why Gabriel would speak with her. (2072-10)

The life as Jesus completed the cycle and established the pattern for all men. The soul again was purified and spiritualized, yet, by having passed through the earth and overcome it, he had control over all his soul's forces. Thus, the Savior.

. . . Hence, as Adam given—the Son of God—so he *must* become that [one who] would be able to take the world, the earth, back to that source from which it came, and *all power* is given in his keeping in the earth that he has overcome: self, death, hell, and the grave even, became subservient unto Him *through* the conquering of self in that made flesh; for, as in the Beginning was the Word, the Word was with God, the Word *was* God, the same was *in* the beginning. The Word came and dwelt among men, the offspring of self in a material world, and the Word *overcame* the world—and hence the world *becomes*, then, as the servant of that [one who] overcame the world. (364-7)

How, why, where was there the need for there to be a resurrection? Why came He into the earth to die, even on the Cross? It has been, then, the fulfillment of promise, the fulfillment of Law, the fulfillment of man's estate:*

*Genesis 3:15. "That man can completely overcome evil—" he fulfilled the promise and showed the way.

else why did He put on flesh and come into the earth in the form of man, but to be One with the Father; to show to man his (man's) divinity, man's relationship to the Maker; to show to man that indeed the Father meant it when He said, "If ye call I will hear. Even though ye be covered with sin, if ye be washed in the blood of the Lamb ye may come back."

Then, though He were the first of man, the first of the sons of God in spirit, in flesh, it became necessary that He fulfill *all* those associations, those connections that were to wipe away in the experience of man that which separates Him from His Maker.

Though man be far afield, then, though he may have erred, there is established that which makes for a closer walk *with* Him, through that one who experienced all those turmoils, strifes, desires, urges that may be the lot of man in the earth. Yet He put on flesh, made *Himself* as naught—even as was promised throughout, to those who walked and talked with God. (5749-6)

Chapter 4
(Genesis 4)

Cain and Abel: Hostile Brothers

The greater significance of Scripture lies not in depicting external history, but in what the outward events represent to the inner man. The rupture between Cain and Abel depicts an ever present condition in man.

It has been understood by most of those who have attained to a consciousness of the various presentations of good and evil in manifested forms, as we have indicated, that the prince of this world, Satan, Lucifer, the Devil—as a soul—made those necessities, as it were, of the consciousness in materiality; that man—or that soul might—become aware of its separation from the God Force.
Hence the continued warring that is ever present in materiality or in the flesh, or the warring—as is termed—between the flesh and the devil, or the warring between the influences of good and evil. (262-89)

The development of the Adamic race was an attempt to crystallize the thought-form projections into God's manner of expressing the Spirit. However the attempt failed. As these five races entered, they began to take on forms that would gratify and satisfy carnal desires.
With the fall and ensuing entrapment and loss of spiritual consciousness in a material world, more souls, or spirit, continued entering this dimension as a "balanc-

ing factor" to the spirit of self-indulgence which was leading many of the Sons of God astray.

Q-4 What was meant by the Sons of the Highest in Atlantis and the second coming of souls to the earth, as mentioned in a Life Reading given through this channel?
A-4 In this period or age, as was seen—there is fault of words here to *project* that as actually *occurs* in the *formations* of that as comes about! There was, with the *will* of that as came into being through the correct channels, of that as created by the Creator, that of the *continuing* of the souls in its projection and projection—see? while in that as was *of* the off-spring, of that as pushed itself *into* form to *satisfy, gratify,* that of the desire of that known as carnal forces of the *senses,* of those created, there continued to be the war one with another, and there were then —*from* the other *sources* (worlds) the continuing entering of those that *would* make for the keeping of the balance, as of the first purpose of the Creative Forces, as it magnifies itself in that given sphere of activity, of that [which] had been *given* the *ability* to *create* with its *own* activity—see? and hence the second, or the *continued* entering of souls into that known as the earth's plane during this period, for that activity as was brought about. (364-7)

Perhaps this "continued entering" by the Sons of God as a balancing factor to avert complete separation through self-indulgence is what is meant when Enoch prophesied, saying, "Behold the Lord comes with ten thousand of his saints." (Jude 1:14)

Their effect as teachers and ministers is shown in the fact that by the time of Seth's son Enos, "men began to call upon the name of the Lord." (Genesis 4:26)

The above reading continues:

Let's *remember* that as was given, in the second, third from Adam, or fourth, or from Amilius, there was "In that day did they *call upon* the name of the Lord"—is right! and ever, when the elements that make for littleness, uncleanness, are crucified in the body, the *Spirit* of the Lord, of God, is present! When these are overbalanced, so that the body (physical), the mental man, the imagination of its heart, is evil, or his purpose is evil, then is that war continuing—as from the beginning. Just the continued warring of those things within self as from the beginning; for with these changes as brought *sin* into the world, with same came the *fruits* of same, or the seed as of sin, which we see in the material world as those things that corrupt good ground, those that corrupt the elements that are of the compounds of those of the first causes, or elementals, and pests are seen—and the like, see? So does it follow throughout all creative forces, that the fruits of that as is active brings that seed that makes for the corrupting of, or the clearing of, in the activative forces of, that *being* acted upon. (364-7)

To the Israelites, Babel was the place where God divided mankind into various nations. (Deuteronomy 32:8) However, the first indication of the fragmentation of the original unity is in Genesis 4, with the murder of Abel and the flight of Cain and Cain's marriage to an unknown outside group.

Cayce indicates these events were taking place 500,000 to 50,000 years before Moses! (877-26)

. . . in the Atlantean land when there were those divisions between those of the Law of One and the Sons of Belial, and the offspring of what was the pure race and those that had projected themselves into creatures that became as the sons of man (as terminology would be) rather than the creatures of God. (1416-1)

57

The following reading discusses the divisions that were taking place. Cayce uses the terms "Sons of Belial" in the reading, but they represent the same activity as "The Children of Cain."

Cayce told this person he had been "firstborn of the sons of men":

When the first of life in flesh form appeared in the earth's plane, this entity was among those making the first appearance in the form of man, or when the development reached such that the universal forces then created the soul man. The entity was among the firstborn of the sons of men. (4609-1)

In the second influx came the Sons of the Highest as bearers of spiritual knowledge. Some were giants, and were sought out by those of the first creation. The reference to "first dwellings" indicates a service also.

When there was the second coming of souls into the earth's plane, this entity was among those who gave the first dwellings for groups. The entity was of giant stature, and was of those who were called Sons of the Highest, for there came many of the first rule that were sought by those peoples. This was before the day of the Flood. (2802-1)

877-26 is a significant reading which defines the separation between the Sons of God and the issues which polarized them.

Hence we find there had been the separating into groups (as we would call them) for this or that phase of activity; and those that were against that MANNER of development.

The Sons of Belial were of one group, or those that sought more the gratifying, the satisfying, the use of material things for self, WITHOUT thought or consideration as to the sources of such nor the hardships in the experiences of others. Or, in other words, as we would term it today, they were those without a standard of morality.

The other group—those who followed the Law of One—had a standard. The Sons of Belial had no standard, save of self, self-aggrandizement. (877–26)

The descendants of Seth kept to the heritage of Amilius, or Adam. Cain is symbolic of the followers of Belial.

A form of non-sexual conception—represented by the creation of Eve from the rib of Adam—was practiced by those souls who were of the Law of One. Through their unity with the Spirit, the innocent and pure in spirit could enter into the earth plane through the channels they established. The Sons of Belial, who were indulging in sexual or carnal forces, were attuned to a more material consciousness. Their spirit had become polluted through their activities in the earth.

Then we find the entity, now known as or called [877], was among the children of the Law of One; entering through the natural sources that had been considered in the period as the means of establishing a family. However, they were rather as a group than as an individual family.

For those who were of the ruling forces were able by choice to create or bring about, or make the channel for the entrance or the projection of an entity or soul, as the period of necessity arose.

Then such were not as households or as families, like we have today, but rather as groups.

Their STANDARD was that the soul was given by the Creator or entered from outside sources INTO the projection of the MENTAL and spiritual self at the given periods. THAT was the standard of the Law of One, but was REJECTED by the Sons of Belial.

But this entity, [877], is the one whom we are to follow in the present; as for its application of those innate tenets, that are a portion of the aroma of the innate being, as it were, or the influence that is as the rate of vibratory force of the entity in its relationships to the universal activity or vibratory forces.

These are the abilities to which the entity may attune self, through all the various phases of its application in those directions in other experiences.

But that was among the first entrances, or the second entrance of the entity FROM the without, into that form which became encased as an entity, an INDIVIDUAL body, see? (877-26)

Later it is recorded that Noah "was pure in his generation," which probably refers to this spiritual manner of producing offspring.

Earliest Developments
The Animal Nature and the Ego

As perfect men separated from the unity and oneness of Spirit, individual awareness, or the ego, evolved. The impact of this was the fragmenting of the Sons of God into scattered groups and clans.

As they moved further and further away from their first estate as spiritual beings, they became dependent upon the material world, rather than the God-Within, for protection, sustenance, and knowledge.

This reading speaks of that development.

In the first, then, we find the necessity of now supplying its own foods, its own protection, its own activities for amusements, for developments, for its associations one with another, and—as given—then selfishness, and the desire to excel, the desire to place self as in control of, in the supervision of, those things or others about same, gradually developed households, groups, clans, masses, then originally—or eventually—in that known as various groups, houses, or nations. (364-12)

The murder of Abel by his self-centered and ego-conscious brother, Cain, is a record of this early development.

Unruly Cain is a personification of that Fallen Spirit which fathered all the divisions and separations between man.

With man's advent into the world, then personalities, individualities began to find expression in *subduing* the earth, and man—with his natural bent—not only attempted to subdue the *earth*, but to subdue one another; and the result was the differences of opinions, the various sects, sets, classes, and races. (3976-8)

The extent to which man became involved in the animal world, or materiality, is suggested in a symbolic way, when it is recorded, "God made for Adam and his wife coats of skin." (Genesis 3:21) This verse might possibly signify the flesh body which gradually became an encasement for the soul.

As to their forms in the physical sense, these were much rather of the nature of thought-forms . . . As these took form, by the gratifying of their own desire for that as builded or added to the material conditions, they became hardened or set—much in the form of the existent human body of the day . . . (364-3)

The coats of skin also signify the self-awareness that resulted from abuses of the physical body, which became a part of an actual evolutionary development, as many of the Sons of God changed their diets from herb and seed to meat.

As for the dress, those in the beginnings were (and the Lord made for them coats) of the skins of the animals. These covered the parts of their person that had become, then, as those portions of their physiognomy that had brought much of the desires that made for destructive forces in their own experience, and these then were of those *about* them that were given as meat, or used as same—that partook of the herbs. (364-11)

Those who had partaken of the animal forces now needed the meat of the animal to sustain their physical bodies. The vegetarian diet was kept by those who had not mixed or indulged, and was the manner imaged by God (Genesis 1:29) for the souls in the beginning.*

These were those same herbs that the seed were to have been for food for the man in self, and only those that partook of same may be called even *clean*—in the present day . . . for these carry all the elements in their natural state. Little of minerals should ever be the properties within the system, save as may be taken through the vegetable forces, save where individuals have so laxed themselves as to require or need that which will make for an even balance of same. (364-11)

Those who "remained clean" and those who indulged in "desires that made for destructive forces" are symbolically represented in Cain and Abel.

*The ideal diet recommended by Cayce included "fish, fowl, and lamb," with proper combinations of vegetables, either cooked or raw.

Cayce never advocated vegetarianism as a universal diet. Apparently because our physical bodies, over many incarnations, have become dependent upon and conditioned to meat as an energy source. To suddenly deny meat to the body could cause great harm. In order to preserve and maintain balance, health, and stability, the return to the Genesis diet must be gradual.

The concept of Sacrifice, which is integral to their story, was also an evolutionary concept at this time, kept by those whom Cayce termed "The Sons of the Law of One."

... in the latter portion of the experience of Amilius [or Adam] was the first establishing of the altars upon which the sacrifices of the field and the forest, and those that were of that [which] *satisfied* the desires of the physical body were builded. (364-4)

The concept of sacrifice was an attempt by those souls who were still spiritually attuned to create a mode of worship which would aid others in re-establishing their relationship to God.

The real sacrifice was disengaging from animal involvements, as is seen in the following from a Life Reading.

The *entity* was among the children of the Law of One, those that were the sons of men, yet of the daughters of the Lord—or those who had become purified of those entanglements in the animal forces that became manifest among many. (1066-1)

Sacrifice was an attempt to lead souls to the realization that they must sacrifice the animal, or carnal desire, or the self-centered earthly ego, which they had builded within themselves.

For, He has given, no sacrifice is acceptable save as of the *desires* of self to be one with Him. (531-5)

The Vocations of Man

Genesis places Cain as the father of those who are in the world. He is the ancestor of the first practitioners of man's three principal vocations: *agriculture* ("And Adah bare Jabal: he was the father of such as dwell in tents, and of such as have cattle," Genesis 4:20); *the arts* ("And his brother's name was Jubal: he was the father of all such as handle the harp and organ," Genesis 4:21); and *science*, and warfare ("And Zillah, she also bare Tubal-Cain, an instructor of every artificer in brass and iron," Genesis 4:22).

With these developments came then the gradual injection of the use of elements from without for protection, as implements with which to protect themselves, which began with the use of *fitting* stone, iron, brass, copper, and those elements known in the present as instruments of warfare, or of building, or of preservation of the various emoluments of individuals. Hence we had also those for ornamentation of the body, ornamentation of the abode, ornamentation of the various surroundings that had to do with the individuals in their various sets, classes, or groups.

These made for such as dwelt in groups in homes or cities, while others made for those as of following the field, or those as of the hunters, or those as of the agriculturists, or those that had herds, and their various necessities that followed with these. (364–12)

Just as the descendants of Cain obtained their vocations through their dependency upon the earth, the children of Seth were to practice man's other vocation: religion. They were to be guided and sustained by that which came from Within, and to live in the manner as the spirit directed.

To what uses, then, did these people in this particular period give their efforts, and in what directions were they active?

As many almost as there were individuals; for, as we find from the records . . . To some there was given the power to become the Sons of God; others were

64

workers in brass, in iron, in silver, in gold; others were made in music, and the instruments of music. (364-10)

The great geniuses of today, whether in the arts, science, agriculture, or religion, reflect the manner in which they, as entities—as souls—partook or developed in the beginning. Their "genius" is the result of a continued involvement with their vocation over many incarnations.

They Were There

One of the most significant factors of the Edgar Cayce Life Readings is in the weight and support they give to a literal approach to the Bible. Cayce stated almost all portions of Scripture can be interpreted on three levels: literal, metaphysical, and spiritual. But for any level to be valid, it must be practical and applicable and able to be coordinated with the others and be "as one, even as the Father, Son, and the Holy Spirit are one." (281-30)

In other words, a literal level must be consistent with our understanding of mental processes and coordinant with spiritual truth as well. Failure to interpret its three-fold meaning is to deny the Bible its intrinsic wholeness. In some mysterious way, to acknowledge as factual those stories which have previously only been studied symbolically, or allegorically—or dismissed as fantasy or unenlightened primitive mythology—is to restore with added depth the indefinable sacredness of this Book of Life. A good example is found in the Tree of Life, with its signficance on both a symbolic and literal plane.

The Tree of Life is found at the beginning and the end of the Bible, in Genesis and Revelation. In Genesis, Man loses the Tree of Life because of his fall. In Revelation, Man regains his access to the Tree.

Symbolically, both trees represent the same principle.

Q–14 What is meant by the tree of life with its twelve kinds of fruit that yielded her fruit every month and the leaves of the tree for the healing of the nations? (Revelation 22:2)

A–14 That as the tree planted by the water of life; that is, as the sturdiness of the purpose of the individual in its sureness in the Christ; and the leaves represent the activities that are as for the healing of all that the individual activities may contact, even in material life. And that it is CONTINUOUS, as by month, as for the purpose, as for the activities. (281–37)

However, in the actual Garden everything was literally pure and pristine, a reflection of those images conceived in the mind of God. Thus, everything, even the trees, carried spiritual meanings.

In 1944, an Iowa housewife was told preceding an incarnation in Egypt as one of the handmaidens who discovered Moses in the ark (Exodus 2:5), she had been near Eden.

. . . we find the entity was in the early, early days, when there was the garden called Eden. There we find the entity was among those who looked on the activities of the mother of mankind. The entity then was among the "things"* and yet was touched in person, was touched in heart, and sought to know the meaning of same, for it saw then fruit, leaves, trees, which had their spiritual meaning in peoples' lives. (5373–1)

The relationship to this suborder ultimately became an issue between the Sons of God, dividing them into two camps.

*The "things" referred to in the above were also described as "automatons" in other readings. These were creatures which were the result of the mating of the Sons of God with the Daughters of Men. (Genesis 6:2; reading 281–24)

A young Unitarian widow was told of her experience in Atlantis.

> In that sojourn, then, we find that [the entity as] Assen-ni was of the children of the Law of One; with the Children of Belial as the negative influence or force among the children of men.
>
> And there was the realization by Assen-ni that those who had been born were, through no fault of their own, being used as creatures for exploitation; and that through the very influence and power of the Children of Belial the Creative Energies were being used for destructive purposes—or as cloaks behind which their activities might be carried on. (1007–3)

The Cain and Abel story and the question it raises, "Am I my brother's keeper?" may be drawn, in part, from the conflicts of this period. The patriarchs of the Bible drew upon the same source to face similar problems as the children of the Law of One thousands of years earlier. The above reading continues:

> Thus those disintegrations were brought about that were so well given in the injunctions later written in the admonitions to Abraham, to Jacob, to Moses, to Elijah, to Joshua, to all the children of promise—of which we have records.
>
> And if the entity will interpret the admonitions of Moses, much of that which is *the inner basic principle* of the entity may be found. (1007–3)

The Descendants of Cain

Two of Cain's ancestors appear in the Life Readings. In a reading given for a seven year old girl, a very interesting reference is made to Tubal-Cain (Genesis 4:22) as "the first son to become perfect to become an associate with those of other activities." Could this mean that the children of Cain had adapted themselves to the world yet still held a sufficient measure of the Light which enabled them to associate with the mixture races whereas the Adamic race was supposed to keep itself separate from the world?

The daughters of Eve are mentioned as well.

Before that we find the entity lived in that period when there were those in the land of the inter-between, or that between the lands then of Eden—that was between the Euphrates, or where the Red Sea, the Dead Sea *now* occupy—was the entity's dwelling land.

There we find the entity was an associate and a companion of one Tubal-Cain, the first of the sons that had been made perfect to become an associate with those of *other* activities in the earth.

The entity withdrew, and made for those activities that brought about that which is the cry of those that are wounded in body, wounded in spirit, wounded in soul.

Then in the name (as would be called) Su-Su-Lu, though it was a trying and a testing experience, the entity gained. For the entity made overtures to those of the daughters of Eve (in person—that Eve of the garden, that Eve who made for the activities). Though the entity then was the seventh, tenth generations, it made overtures in *person*—in the age at those periods.

In the present experience we will find the entity seeking the association, desiring the association of those much its elder. Not that the periods of its own childhood, not that the periods of the recreation and all developments are not a portion of it, but periods when the tales, the counsels, the imaginations of those of elderly years are sought by the entity.

Do not forbid, but *do* direct. (1179-2)

Cain's progeny also appear in a reading for a young boy, thirteen years old, an invalid since birth. He was told his condition was karmic and originated during the time of Lamech (Genesis 4:19–24)

The reading closes with an indication of the harmful effects the descendants of Cain had upon this entity. Truly was this the line that caused God "to repent that man was made." (Genesis 6:6)

. . . we find the entity was in the period when there were those changes in the sons of Tubal-Cain, when Lamech made for those choices of the first beginnings of when *man* as man partook of those things that made for the multiplicity, or when polygamy began among those peoples. [Genesis 4:19] This brought to the entity during the experience that of disorder, disturbance, the unfavorable expressions of many about the entity; and bringing those experiences that have builded for disorders in the experience. (693–3)

Lamech's actions can be viewed as a continuation of the effects from the negative spirit manifested in Cain.

Adam Reincarnated: Enoch

And Enoch walked with God, and he was not for God took him. As [were] many of those in those first years, in this land, this experience. (364–10)

Enoch is also one of the incarnations Cayce attributed to Jesus in his development as The Christ. The readings also suggest, as in the above, Enoch is representational of many in the earth at that time who had retained their spiritual and mental attunement and were not fully enmeshed in matter.

Man in his natural state, the readings have said, is soul, or spirit.

Although not much is stated about Enoch in the Bible, the readings do give a few illuminating references.

Enoch acted as a prophet who sought to give warnings about the impending Deluge.

Read the Scripture pertaining to the days of Noah, the law proclaimed by Enoch (found mostly in Jude and in the early chapters of Genesis). (3653-1)

. . . Enoch as he warned the people. (3054-4)

He bestowed blessings and recommendations as well as warnings.

Again it was manifested in Enoch, who oft sought to walk and talk with that divine influence; with the abilities . . . to find self in the varied realms of awareness, yet using the office of relationships as a channel through which blessings might come, as well as [through which] recommendations and warnings might be indicated to others. (2072-4)

The possible extent of Enoch's activities is suggested through a tradition that links his name with Hermes. Hermes, for long ages, has been considered the architect of the Great Pyramid of Cheops. Manly Hall, in his *Encyclopedia of Mosaic Heremetics, Rosicrucian Symbolic Philosophy,* in his commentary of Hermes states that many investigators believe Hermes is the same entity whom the Jews refer to as Enoch.

Enoch, in reading 5749-14, is included as one of the major incarnations in the development of the soul who became the man Jesus. Occasional references in other readings indicate Jesus had an incarnation in Egypt under the name Hermes. Further information in the readings, parallel with traditions maintained by the Jews, will strengthen the view that these, Enoch and Hermes, are one and the same.

Pyramid Builders

According to the Edgar Cayce readings on the pre-historical period of ancient Egypt, the high priest, Ra-

Ta, and Hermes directed the construction of the Great Pyramid at Gizeh.

> Then with Hermes and Ra . . . there began the building of that now called Gizeh . . . that was to be the Hall of the Initiates of that sometimes referred to as the White Brotherhood. (5748-5)

Q-5 What was the date of the actual beginning and ending of the construction of the Great Pyramid?
A-5 Was one hundred years in construction. Begun and completed in the period of Araaraatt's time, with Hermes and Ra.
Q-6 What was the date B.C. of that period?
A-6 10,490 to 10,390 before the Prince [of Peace] entered into Egypt. (5748-6)

The meaning of the word ENOCH is *Initiator*. The Edgar Cayce information on the Great Pyramid definitely states its purpose was to serve as a hall of initiation.

Another tradition which would link Hermes and Enoch is found in the Kaballah.

Josephus in his *Antiquities of the Jews* (quoted in the Kaballah) states there is a legend that Adam was forewarned of the Flood. Seth, Adam's surviving son, erected two pillars on which he inscribed the keys to the science and philosophy taught by Adam. Enoch, who also knew of the impending Deluge, became concerned that the knowledge would be lost through this calamity. Therefore he constructed an underground temple with nine vaults. In the final vault were the two pillars upon which, in allegorical symbols, the secret teachings were preserved.

A similar activity is ascribed to Hermes by Edgar Cayce.

The readings show the constructor of the Great Pyramid, Hermes, designed a secret room known as The

Hall of Records, which is as yet undiscovered. In this, according to Edgar Cayce, are placed the ancient teachings of the Law of One as well as a history of Atlantis. Thus we have a parallel between this activity of Hermes and the vaults dug by Enoch.

This question relates to the Hall of Records:

Q-2 Give in detail what the sealed room contains.
A-2 A record of Atlantis from the beginnings of those periods when the Spirit took form or began the encasements in that land, and the developments of the peoples throughout their sojourn, [together] with the record of the first destruction, and the changes that took place in the land; with the record of the *sojournings* of the peoples to the varied activities in other lands; and a record of the meetings of all the nations or lands for the activities in the destructions that became necessary with the final destruction of Atlantis; and the buildings of the Pyramid of Initiation; [together] with who, what, where would come the opening of the records that are as copies from the sunken Atlantis . . . (378-16)

Chapter 5

The Deluge: Division and Dissent

The division and conflict between those Cayce called "Sons of the Law of One" and the "Children of Belial" intensified as it progressed. It began thousands of years before Adam, and has continued into the present.

When the serpent was cursed in Genesis 3:15, he was told that his posterity and that of Eve's would always be at war with each other, and that hers would ultimately triumph.

This is a spiritual law, Cayce states. Those who do good and have the ideal of brotherly love and service to God will always be opposed by and in conflict with those who are motivated only by selfish ends, material gain, and sensuous gratification.

In the days of Noah, this conflict brought world-wide destruction.

... we find these as the Sons of the Creative Force as manifest in their experience looking upon those changed forms, or the daughters of men, and there crept in those pollutions, of polluting themselves with those mixtures that brought contempt, hatred, bloodshed, and those that build for desires of self *without* respects of *others'* freedom, others' wishes—and there began, then, in the latter portion of this period of development, that [which] brought about . . . dissenting and divisions among the peoples in the lands. (364-4)

One of the issues which divided the Sons of God (or Adam) and the Sons of Belial (or Cain) was their relationship to the suborder of "things" or automatons—creatures which were a result of the mixture of the Sons of God with the Daughters of Men.

The "things" were Sons of God who were cut off from the spiritual consciousness, and trapped in imperfect and incomplete forms. The Sons of Belial cultivated them, and used them for the rendering of certain tasks—slaves of the powerful.

Q–2 What is meant by automatons who labored in that experience?
A–2 They were the offspring of the Sons of God with the Daughters of Men, or vice versa. (281-44)

The Bible describes much of the spiritual awareness of that period.

And God saw that the wickedness of man was great in the earth, and that every imagination of the thoughts of his heart was only evil continually.

And it repented the Lord that he had made man on the earth, and it grieved him at his heart. (Genesis 6:5–6)

The following interpretations help clarify its meaning

The heart, of course, here referred to, is not the physical organ, but the purpose, the desire that is to be attained. (2283–1)

. . . for, as has been said, "repent that man was ever made." Why? "For the purpose and intent of Man is to satisfy earthly desires of the flesh rather than that of the manifesting of My Spirit in [the] earth's plane." (139–9)

More detail is supplied in the following:

With the continued disregard of those that were keeping the pure race and the pure peoples, of those that were to bring all these laws as applicable to the Sons of God, man brought in the destructive forces as used for the peoples that were to be the rule, that combined with those natural resources of the gases, of the electrical forces, made in nature and natural form the first of the eruptions that awoke from the depth of the slow cooling earth, and that portion now near what would be termed the Sargasso Sea first went into the depths. With this there again came that egress of peoples that aided, or attempted to assume control, yet carrying with them *all* those forms of Amilius, that he gained through that as for signs, for seasons, for days, for years. Hence we find in those various portions of the world even in the present day, some form of that as *was* presented by those peoples in *that* great *development* in this, the Eden of the world. (364-4)

Cayce indicates that the Flood as we know it through the Old Testament was in actuality the second of three great catastrophies which destroyed Atlantis—or Posei-da:*

. . . before this we find when the ruling force of Poscida was before the gates of the mighty waters that in ages back submerged this plain. (4228-1)

The negative activity of this period, and the destruction which followed, established a symbol, or pattern, which has forever held true in man's experiences.

For as has been given from the beginning, the deluge was not a myth (as many would have you believe)

*See Edgar Evans Cayce, *Edgar Cayce on Atlantis.*

but a period when man had so belittled himself with the cares of the world, with the deceitfulness of his own knowledge and power, as to require that there be a return to his dependence wholly—physically and mentally—upon Creative Forces. (3653-1)

Atlantis was convulsed by three separate destructions which occurred over a long period of time—thousands of years! The second destruction is the one we know as the Deluge.

Symbolically, Noah represents the activity of all the Sons of Light who, through their attunement with Creative Force, or God, took warning of the impending disaster, made adequate preparation, and escaped, settling in all parts of the world.

In the latter portion of same, we find as *cities* were builded, more and more rare became those abilities to call upon rather the forces in nature to supply the needs for those of bodily adornment, or those of the needs to supply the replenishing of the wasting away of the physical being; or hunger arose, and with the determinations to set again in motion, we find there—then Ani,* in those latter periods, ten thousand seven hundred (10,700) years before the Prince of Peace came —again was the bringing into force that to *tempt,* as it were, nature—in its storehouse—of replenishing the things—that of the *wasting* away in the mountains, then into the valleys, then into the sea itself, and the fast disintegration of the lands, as well as of the peoples—save those that had escaped into those distant lands. (364-4)

---

*Ani is mentioned several times in *Myths and Legends of Ancient Egypt* by Lewis Spence.

If the geneology in Genesis 5 is literal then Methuselah was alive at the time of the Deluge.

The readings show the lifespan in those days was indeed incredible.

The days upon the earth then were counted in the tens, the fifties, and the hundreds, besides the days or weeks or years in the present. Or, the LIFE existence of the entity, as compared to the present, would be years instead of weeks; or, in that experience to live five to six to seven hundred years was no more than to live to the age of fifty, sixty, or seventy years in the present. (1968-2)

Cayce described in a Life Reading for a prominent brain surgeon and metaphysician an experience as "the eighth from Adam." This could mean that the surgeon (1851) had been Methuselah.

As a descendant of Adam, he, too, was concerned with the study, interpretation, and preservation of the records made by the children of the Law of One in Atlantis and preserved by Enoch,

Again we find the entity, before that, was in the Egyptian land during the very early periods.

For the entity was the eighth from Adam, and in the days of the exodus and the periods of understanding through those activities; journeying more from what is now the Chaldean than the Egyptian land, though spending many of the periods in the activities through which the records were set as for things that were, that were to be—these become a part of the study of the entity throughout those periods.

Hence oft the entity may lose self in those things that are found there. For, as that was the interpreting of the earth as it was, as it is, as it is to be, so came those activities to preserve same for the seeker to know his relationships to the past, the present, and the future, when counted from the material standpoint.

And as the entity sought in those experiences to make time and space, as well as patience, the realms that express the universality of the Force called God, so may THIS become in the present experience that in which the entity may excel—in giving assurance to those who seek their closer understanding of the relationships one to another. (1851–1)

The Bible says God repented he made man. (Genesis 6:6) Edgar Cayce interpreted this to mean a change in heart and a new plan for man's salvation.

The following comments are taken from the Bible class record.

"To repent means to change the mind because of regret or dissatisfaction. God decided to give man a new opportuinty, or a new method, for saving himself. Because man was so wicked, God cut his life span to 120 years. The only hope for man to extricate himself from the flesh was to die at a younger age, and get a new start by being reborn. This was God's way of making man aware of a new opportunity. How terrible it would be today if we kept living for thousands of years!"

This reading compares man's lifespan then and now.

What was the length of life then? Nearly a thousand years. What is your life today? May it not be just as He had given, just as He had indicated to those peoples, just as He did to the lawgiver, just as He did to David—first from a thousand years to a hundred and twenty, then to eighty? Why? Why? The sin of man is his desire for self-gratification.

What nations of the earth today vibrate to those things that they have and are creating in their own land, their own environment? Look to the nations where the span of life has been extended from sixty to eighty-four years. You will judge who is serving God. These are judgments. These are the signs to those who seek to know, who will study the heavens, who will analyze the elements, who will know the heart of man, they that seek to know the will of the Father for themselves answer, "Lord, here am I, use me, send me where I am needed." (3976-29)

Noah

The Deluge is both symbolic and literal. Noah was also an actual entity.

In a noteworthy Life Reading, a four year old child was told he had been Thomas Cambell, founder of the Cambellite movement, Elisha the prophet, and the ancient patriarch of the Deluge.

For, before *that* the entity was that one to whom was entrusted man's advent into the world—Noah!

For this we find those weaknesses. Then, not as one refraining from those, but beware ever of any strong drink or fruit of the vine passing the lips of THIS entity—through these early periods, especially. (2547-1)

Although Noah was found naked and drunk in his tent after the Deluge, before the Flood it is written he and his family were "perfect in their generations." (Genesis 6:9)

Noah and his family still adhered to the tenets of the Law of One. They had not yet "broken the faith"—as this one had . . .

Before that we find the entity was in the Atlantean land during those periods when there were the separations of the peoples from the high and the low estates of the varied developments that were in that period of man's experience in the earth, when there were the Sons of the High; or as given in Holy Writ, "The Sons of God looked upon the Daughters of Men."

The *entity* was among the Sons of God, yet looking upon the Daughters of Men and making of self in those associations those periods when faith was broken with others, and when there was the belittling of the tenets and the truths in the *powers* that had been given among those peoples for the manifesting of that which would cleanse their souls that they might be one with the Creative Forces in this *material* world and in the spiritual forces also. (518-1)

Noah and his group, no doubt, refrained from mixing with the creatures who were combinations of the thought-forms projected by the Sons of Belial and the descendents of Cain.

They were perfect in their day and generation. As individual entities they had chosen virtue in every form in relationship to things, conditions, and personalities in the earth. (3653-1)

The eight souls were saved for a definite purpose—to preserve the consciousness that had been brought into the earth through Adam and the followers of the Law of One, and to continue the spiritual and mental evolution of mankind.

For the entity was among those eight souls saved for a definite purpose, and brought that influence in the earth that is today that source from which spiritual and mental advance has been kept toward that more commonly termed the more civilized groups or individuals. (2627-1)

Cayce's commentary to the Bible class follows:

"Noah is the next man after Enoch who walked with God. So God chose him as the channel through which His new method would be used. It is indicated that at the time of the Flood, Noah was the only man living who had come down in a direct line from Seth without contamination through intermarriage with the thought-form projections. All flesh was polluted. Only Noah and his family were allowed to have a part in the New Dispensation."

Although it is written Noah was perfect in his generations, we have evidence later (Genesis 9:21–25) he was not perfect, mentally or spiritually. Even though he had come down in a perfect line, his anger and resentment at Ham show he was not free from sin. This also shows how powerful our own anger can be in its effect upon others. Noah's anger produced a curse on all Ham's descendants. Our own words and actions create similar conditions. They bring fruits after their own kind.

Cayce continues:

"The Bible says, 'There were giants in those days.'

"Many of the myths which have been handed down to us are based on truth from the beginning. With the intermarriage among the various projections of the physically strong, no wonder there were giants. They had superhuman ability, but lacked spiritual awareness. They were intent upon increasing their physical strength without taking thought to its spiritual source.

Noah's sons must have married their own close relations. All others were contaminated—or mixtures."

A literal reading of the Bible indicates the Flood covered the southern portion of Europe, western Asia, and northern Africa. Yet in the eastern portion of Asia, in South America, Egypt, and Yucatan, myths have been preserved about a great flood and the salvation of one family.

Did the Flood really cover the whole face of the earth, as stated in Scripture? Or did similar experiences occur within all the five races at different periods?

The readings predict the discovery of ancient Atlantean records in Egypt and Yucatan which will reveal the answers to these questions.

How did Noah gather all the animals? The Bible class records show an interesting comment made by Cayce:

"Animals are much closer to God in spirit than we are. They sense any great change that is imminent. Perhaps they came to him."

In the Ark

An interesting group of readings follow involving entities who were with Noah on the ark.

Cayce began this reading for a young Kentucky housewife by commenting:

What an unusual record—and one of those who might be termed as physically the mothers of the world! For the entity was one of those in the ark.

In giving the interpretations of the records here, we find that there is much from which to choose. But these we choose with the desire and purpose to be the means of help to the entity in better fulfilling those purposes for which it has entered the earth's plane in varied periods of its experience.

For the entity has appeared when there were new revelations to be given. And again it appears when there are new revelations to be made.

May the entity so conduct its mind, its body, and its purposes, then, as to be a channel through which such messages may come that are needed for the awakenings in the minds of men as to the necessity for returning to the search for their relationship with the Creative Forces or God.

Will this entity see such again occur in the earth? Will it be among those who may be given those directions as to how, where, the elect may be preserved for the replenishing again of the earth?

Remember, not by water—for it is the mother of life in the earth—but rather by the element fire.

As to whether or not the entity will be among those in the earth when the changes again come, will depend upon the entity's preparation of self. (3653-1)

Cayce described for her experiences in Lemuria, the period of the Judges in Israel; in the Holy Land during the time of Muhammad; and in the South during the War Between the States, as well as in the era of the Flood. He told her she had always been in the earth during times of great change and when new revelations were being made.

Edgar Cayce described her experience during the Deluge thus:

Next we find that the entity entered in those periods when the littleness of man had come up as a stench before the throne of mercy and grace, or the Creative Forces.

The entity was among the peoples not of the lineage of Noah, but of those later known as the Hittites. Then the entity gave expressions to that same experience that was materially manifested in Mu, and the entity—as the wife of a son of Noah—became among the eight souls in the ark, in the preparation and in the endurance thereof, and in those experiences gained in the activities through the earth's influence.

The name then was Maran. From that sojourn there is much experienced in the present in the entity's liking of the history of the early ages of man, of those experiences that are the promptings for the souls and minds of individuals, rather than the material things.

At times the entity is berated by others for being rather in that mind of "Don't care" than in that of a practical, everyday life.

Hence the entity is a "sensitive." Read the Scripture pertaining to the days of Noah, the law proclaimed by Enoch (found mostly in Jude and in the early chapters of Genesis). Here is one entity who may write, not automatic but rather inspirational writing, shutting itself away and attuning itself by very distant music, and especially bells. For, under such an inspiration—not as a means of doing other than attuning the inner self—the entity may write inspirationally of things pertaining to mental and spiritual aspects of individuals grasping for attunement to the divine. (3653-1)

The Family of Japeth

Through a series of readings members of a New Hampshire family discovered they had all known each other in the ark.

The New Hampshire man (2726), a dairy farmer, was told he had been Japeth and that his present wife (2425) had been his wife.

Japeth's wife, Rezepatha, was pregnant when she entered the ark and gave birth during the deluge. The child which was born to them was also reincarnated in the present, but not a part of their family and, indeed, unknown to the farmer or his wife.

A nurse which the family had hired to watch over their children was told in her reading she had been her mistress' mother during this early period of history.

This interesting story begins with the father—Japeth.

Before that we find there was the experience of the greater period of development for the entity in the material world.

For we find the entity, as the son of Noah, chose

the better way for transmitting in fact, in activity, to his peoples after the sojourn in the ark, not only the needs for the establishing of homes but of home altars, and the uniting of those home altars in a group, a nation, a national activity.

The name then was Japeth. In the experience the beauty of the companionship, of the entity's activities, not only before but after the period of preparation and throughout the sojourn, found its expression and activity in that channel through which the hope of the world did and has come again.

Thus in the present may the entity, with those associations, those companionships, bring—has brought —an activity which may add to that harmony in the material world, that will again SING—as the entity did through that period of activity—the realm of the infinite made manifest in man's heart, man's purpose, man's joy.

Leave aside, then, those things that would easily beset, knowing thy purpose and thy ideal, thy IDEAL —physically, mentally, spiritually. Know that all that takes place or that takes form in the mind is prompted either by the spirit of truth or the spirit of rebellion. Which WILL YE choose?

Know the ideal, then, must be as was manifest in Him, who gave, "If ye love me, ye will keep my commandments—and I will come and abide with thee." That promise is in spirit, is in truth.

Hence those as this entity may bring, with its companionship—as did bring, as did keep the home fire bright to the altar of the Lord—may bring again to man, in those activities in the earth, that of a joy. Not easy from the material angle, unless that ideal is held aloft in spirit, in mind, in material things. (2627-1)

His present wife was then his companion in the ark.

85

Q. What have been my associations in the past with, first, my wife, [2425]?
A. The greater experience, the greater advancement is in that innate or soul urge from that period in the ark. (2627-1)

His wife's life was described as follows:

Before that the entity was in that activity when there were those preparations for changes being wrought in the relationships of Creative Forces with the sons of men.

The entity was among those, or that one chosen by Japeth as the companion in the ark.

With [the] relationships to that activity, the entity finds within self the visions of changes, in the relationships that are again soon to be established by and through the elements themselves in their dealing with men and Creative Forces or God's Laws.

The name then was Rezepatha. (2425-1)

An English nurse, who had been employed to watch over the couple's young children, was told in her reading that she had been Japeth's mother-in-law—and had helped prepare her daughter Rezepatha for the responsibility she was to bear.

Before that, during the early activities when there were those preparations for the preserving of man's activity in the earth—the entity was the mother of that entity who was the companion of Japeth, when there were the preparations of the ark.

The entity was that one who contributed to those abilities for that daughter who in her associations brought to the earth the line of activity, the purposes to hold to love as well as purpose.

86

The name then was Lapeth. (2625-1)

The nurse then asked about past life connections, first with the wife:

Q-1 What has been my former connection with the following and how may I best help them in the present? First, [2425]?
A-1 Oft there have been the associations. The greater was in the experiences when the entity was the mother of that entity now known as [2425], during those periods just before what is called the Flood . . . In the present, as has been and may be gathered from paralleling the lives, not only of the offspring in the present—there may be brought that consistency of purpose, that beauty of living for a purpose.
Q-2 Mr. [2627]?
A-2 In the experience that has been indicated—the period of the Flood.
Q-4 Should I continue making my home with [2425]?
A-4 By all means! (2625-1)

Three years after this series of readings, a middle-aged Pennsylvania stenographer was told in a previous life she had been the child of Japeth and Rezepatha.

Before that we find the entity was in the land when there were those preparations that man would not be wholly destroyed but how that the Father-God warned Noah to build the ark and to gather his sons and their families. The entity was one born in the ark during those periods, for the wife of Japeth, the son of Noah, was heavy with child, and it was born during those periods in the ark.

The entity knows, then, the escape, knows the way innately, and that it is only through the hands, the arms of God. Keep that eternal. Do give that to thy fellowman. (5367-1)

The youngest child of the New Hampshire couple was told he was among the first-born after the Deluge.

Before that the entity was in the earth in the early periods of man's activity, when there were children born to the sons of Noah.

The entity was among the first of the groups born in the earth after the deluge or Flood and the resettling in the lands of that period.

Then in the name Pelus, the entity was among those who made rules, laws, and regulations for activities under which there was agreement by the various groups of its own peoples, in their separations, as to the records of how there were to be the settlings and where and what would be the privileges of individuals.

Thus we find those activities leading to the needs for the entity being first mindful of the health, then the opportunity in the training for law and public service. (5008–1)

Japeth's Prayer

Following his descent from the ark, Noah made an altar and sacrificed. He must have been moved to do something in order to show appreciation for being saved.

After the sacrifice, and the promise given to him through the rainbow, Noah began to till the fields. (Genesis 9:20)

Included in this answer is an insight into some of the problems and conditions which faced Japeth and Noah as they left the ark.

The young farmer asked:

Q–1 In farming, what should my emphasis be on?
A–1 Each product is to supply certain elements to the body of man; not by man's changing same, but that purpose the Creator gave it as food, as a supply to

man's physical need IN even a changing world. Thus the stress should be upon each product being given ITS opportunity for fulfilling its mission in relationship to man; or the study of the soil as to how BETTER to produce grasses, vegetables, fruits, berries, or the like; or to supply the elements in the animal kingdom—as of the pig or the cow; that its flesh, its milk, may have those elements NECESSARY for supplying to men that which has its spiritual value and not in a cantankerous or a diffusing manner. For, as man assimilates in the mind, so it assimilates in the spirit. That is why the entity in its experience with its associates when leaving the ark, found it necessary for taking these things into consideration—as to those very necessary elements. (2627-1)

In closing his reading, Cayce recalled a prayer for 2627 which indicates Japeth's realization of his relationship with God:

"Let thy meditation oft be that even as ye did upon the hills in Ararat:

"Lord, Thou art Maker of heaven and earth. Thou hast preserved Thy servant for a purpose in the earth. Thou hast given me, today, opportunities. Help me, O God, to choose the right way; that I may ever be a channel of blessings to others, pointing the way ever to Thee."

We are through for the present. (2627-1)

The Beginning of the Rainbow and End of the Thought-Forms

The following is an interpretation of the meaning of the rainbow in Genesis 9:12–17. It signifies a state of consciousness arising from a period of trial and testing which has been successfully met.

. . . the promises of the Divine that were and are written in the rainbow of the sky, when the cloud has passed, are the same as written in the lives of individuals that they, too, who are in the closer walk with the Creative Forces, may see their sign, their colors, and KNOW whereunto they have attained in THEIR relationship with Creative Energies or God. (1436-2)

No matter what man may bring upon himself in a material sense, he can rely on God's laws and promises to remain the same.

The Flood resulted in the cleansing of the earth. The negative, spiritually polluted thought-forms which had been created by the Sons of God were destroyed in the Deluge. The cataclysm marked the end of an era. Abraham starts the new.

Thence we find the entity passing through those experiences becoming rather aware, with the sons of those activities in the experiences when all thought-forms in matter were put away—through the experience of Noah. (257-201)

Apparently the Deluge marked the end of the centaurs, satyrs, cyclops, harpies, and mermaids, and the other creatures who are now preserved in the mythology of the world.

Some brought about monstrosities, as those if its (that entity's) association by its projection with its association with beasts of various characters. Hence those of the Styx, satyr, and the like; those of the sea, or mermaid; those of the unicorn, and those of the various forms—these projections of what? The abilities in the *psychic* forces (psychic meaning, then of the mental *and* the soul . . .) (364-10)

Not all the thought-forms partook of the animal. Cayce described many as entangled in the plant and mineral kingdoms as well. These too were destroyed.

. . . those who were physically entangled in the animal kingdom with appendages, with cloven hooves, with four legs, with portions of trees, with tails, with scales, with those various things that thought-forms or evil had so indulged in as to separate the purpose of God's creation of man, as man—not as animal . . . (2072-8)

The Egyptian sphinx is a monument to these pre-Deluge creations.

These may be seen in a different manner presented in many of the various sphinxes, as called, in other portions of the land—as the lion with the man, the various forms of wing, or characterizations in their various developments. These were as [the] presentations of those projections that had been handed down in the various developments of that which becomes man— as in the present. (5748-6)

Many souls, like Noah, were manifesting the higher awareness. They heeded the warnings, made adequate preparations, and escaped the destruction.

The Foundation of a New Age

The exodus from Atlantis carried souls both East and West—into Egypt and Yucatan, and other parts of the world.

The Sons of God, who had entered with Adam, projecting into five parts of the earth at once, established great civilizations. The activities in the Egyptian civilization are most vividly described in the readings. Both

Sons of God—the descendants of Adam—and the surviving thought-form races migrated to these centers.

The work of the Sons of the Law of One—or descendants of Adam—was concerned with maintaining and developing a record of the God-consciousness in the earth. They were also concerned with getting the earthbound entities to relate to mental, spiritual, and physical patterns that would re-establish their relationship with spiritual forces.

Before that the entity was in the Egyptian land when there were those preparations for purifying the body and those activities that enabled men to put away [the] appendages, that man in the experience inherited through the pushing of spirit into matter to become materially expressive—and thus [had] brought the necessity of man being materialized in the earth as the perfect body in Adam [in the beginning]. (3333-1)

Following are a few brief descriptions of the work that was being done in Egypt.

. . . there arose the needs for the Temple of Sacrifice, where entities, individuals, might offer themselves for the purification of their bodies, that they first might be channels through which there might come entities, souls, manifesting in the earth with the entire activity of body, mind, soul . . . And with these expressions there were those who chose the activities that were set in motion for the purifying of their bodies, that there might be the purifying of physical conditions which had been and were being affected by the emotional forces, or the carnal influences about them in the experience. (281-43)

Cayce described the Temple of Sacrifice as the equivalent of a modern day hospital, where surgery was performed to remove the appendages—such as scales, hooves, claws, and horns—from the thought-form bodies.

The passage of individuals . . . through the experiences in the Temple of Sacrifice was much as would be in the hospitalization, or a hospital of the present day, when there have become antagonistic conditions within the physical body, such as to produce tumors, wens, warts, or such.

Magnify this into the disturbances which were indicated or illustrated in conditions where there was the body or figure of the horse, or the head of the horse with the body of man; or where there were the various conditions indicated in the expressions by the pushing of spirit into physical matter until it became influenced by or subject to same. Such influences we see in the present manifested as habits, or the habit forming conditions.

Then there are, or were the needs for the attempts to operate, as well as to adhere to diets and activities to change the natures of the individuals, that their offspring, as well as themselves, might bring forth that which was in keeping with—or a pattern of—those influences in which there were SOULS or spirits with the idea, or ideal, of seeking light.

For, how is it termed in the record? That the heart and purpose of man is to do evil! (281-44)

A highly developed form of spiritual, and psychological counseling was done in the Temple Beautiful, also in Egypt.

The Temple of Sacrifice was a physical experience, while the Temple Beautiful was rather of the mental, in which there was the spiritualization—not idolizing, but crystallizing of activities or services to a special purpose—or specializing in preparation for given offices of activity.

Hence from same has arisen a great many of the signs, the symbols, the various influences that have had and may have a part in influencing peoples and individuals . . . toward activities for greater expansions, greater developments. (281–43)

In the present when evil has taken hold, it forms itself into those influences that are called habits, or inclinations, or intents; and it is necessary to eliminate these from the purposes and aims and desires of individuals.

So were the experiences through those activities is the Temple of Service of what is known as the Temple of Sacrifice; sacrificing self that the spirit, the purpose, the love of God might be made manifest through the individual. (281–44)

When the holocaust was over, a new era in the evolution of man began. Temple services such as in Egypt laid the foundation.

The physical pattern brought with the Adamic line was now firmly established. No longer would great monstrosities or unusual mixtures be created. The era of occult projections (via mind and spirit force) was over. All souls who desired to enter the earth's plane had to manifest through the natural channels provided through the sexual union of man and woman.

The sex-force, which had tempted man and led to his entanglement in matter, would have to be purified and creative in order to lift him out.

A new phase of development follows the Deluge. If the pre-Deluge era relates to the period of establishing physical evolutionary patterns for man, the ensuing period relates to the building of Mind, or mental awareness. Only through a purified Life-force enlivening the mind of man and his senses could a higher awareness be developed—as the recipient of this reading was counseled:

Think no evil, speak no evil, hear no evil, and as the Truth flows as a stream of life through the mind in all its phases or aspects of same, so will it purify and revivify and rejuvenate the body. (294-183)

Just as the ideal pattern for the physical body was established, or evolved in the phase preceding the Deluge, the following cycle relates to the development of the perfect Mind.

For, that which leads to the Christ is the Mind. And the mind's unfoldment may be that indicated from Abraham to the Christ. (281-63)

But before Abraham, there is Babel.

Chapter 6

The Tower of Babel

As the Sons of God multiplied in the earth, the size of their groups increased, and they eventually became nations.

Thus when man began to defy God in the earth and the confusion arose which is represented in the Tower of Babel—these are [the] representation of what was then the basis, the beginnings of nations. Nations were set up then in various portions of the land, and each group, one stronger than another, set about to seek their gratifications. (3976-29)

The developments represented in Genesis 11 occurred over many thousands, if not millions of years, and originated in pre-Adamic civilizations. Moses, in order to present an easily grasped and comprehensible picture, told his history as a continuous, chronological sequence. Actually the events symbolized in Cain and Abel, the Flood, and the Tower were occurring simultaneously and were overlapping events. These stories depict the same phenomena, told from different points of view—the loss of the spiritual consciousness and its effect upon the Sons of God.

. . . commenting upon the subject *Destiny of the Soul:*
As man finds himself in the consciousness of a material

world, materiality has often, in the material-minded, blotted out the consciousness of a soul. (262–89)

Before Babel, the whole world "spoke one language with few words." (Genesis 11:1)

The disruption of communications of all natures between men is what? Remember the story, the allegory if ye choose to call it such, of the Tower of Babel. (5757–1)

Edgar Cayce's Bible class lessons contain several thoughtful conceptions. The following is a composite of the presentation.

"Were the people conscious of evil while building the Tower? They must have been aware of doing something that deep within themselves they knew was not necessary to do. They felt they had to rely upon their own physical abilities to build material defenses against another disaster. They were acting in direct opposition to the promise that there would no longer be any wholesale destruction by Flood.

"They were afraid of being scattered, and the very thing they hoped would prevent it actually caused it to happen.

"Because they were of one mind, to build in the material, God saw the power of their united imaginations could and would build such a barrier that they would never find Heaven.

"As they built, they became aware of God. The Spirit entered into their consciousness and changed their attitude toward the work. No wonder they became confused.

"God's laws are such that their own material building began to confuse them. It is the same today. We can go so far in the material and no further. We defeat our own selves.

"Their concept of Heaven was a place high up. They were looking outside of themselves for it. They were about to start the whole process of thought-form creation all over again. They had to realize, through long ages of suffering and learning obedience (just as we must) that the real building of the Tower is within the individual, not outside. The preparation must be within."

The time arrived, even in the Adamic line, when the people no longer wholly believed in spiritual truths or universal law. They began to worship their own physical abilities, their own individual prowess and powers, and began to act independently of the Spirit.

Once this pattern was established, trouble and tribulation resulted.

Yet man in his greed, in his own selfishness, has set himself so oft at naught by the very foolishness of his own wisdom.

For the soul had understanding before he partook of the flesh in which the choice was to be made. The choice, or the road, or the path, once taken, then the end thereof was (and is) tribulation, toil, misunderstanding. And this expression came into such measures that *there arose the periods when man came as one* and said, "We will *build*, we will go to now and make those conditions that will prevent any such confusion again among men."

And then came the diversity of tongues and confusion arose. For the very selfishness of man had brought [about] this confusion, this defiance to a God of love, of mercy, of patience, in such a measure that He gave that expression, "There is nothing beyond the scope of man's ability unless he misinterpret his brother's words." (262–96)

In a subsequent reading, a clarification was asked.

Q–3 Please explain . . . what is meant by "any such confusions" referred to when it was said, "We will build, we will go to now and make those conditions that will prevent *any such confusions again* among men."

Why did they think a Tower would help?

A–3 The Tower was after the flood. This is very simple—to reach above. Why do you build houses? Why do you build boats, those things that become "above the flood"? It was just the same! Same concept—that it might reach even to that which would *not* be destroyed by flood again. (262–99)

If Cayce is correct, this entity was an ancestor of those who erected the Tower.

Before that the entity lived in the earth during those periods when the peoples were separated that prepared for the preserving of the activities in the earth.

The entity was the son of Ham (Canaan) that laughed at the weakness of the grandfather [Genesis 9]. Thus the entity was one of those who occupied the ark, or was in the ark during that period.

After the journeys in the ark, the entity set out activities in definite conditions for the establishing of groups in various portions of the land.

Thus things that have to do with mechanical things are innately of interest. And the entity gathers those peculiar things or oddities about itself in one respect or another.

As to the abilities of the entity in the present . . . the application of self should be in writing of the peculiarities, the oddities of various groups and in their manner of worship in various portions of the earth. (3345–1)

In this Life Reading we have a record of activities around the Tower of Babel. It indicates the pattern is still the same today.

. . . the entity was active when there were those first separations of the sons of those who were saved at the periods when the ark settled upon Ararat, and when the divisions arose just before the activities in the Tower of Babel.

We find that the entity attempted to create the better relationships with the various groups of individuals, and those who sought to make for disturbances that brought dissensions among the sons of Noah.

For the entity attempted to carry on those tenets and conditions which had been presented by his grandfather Noah in that period. Yet the entity was over ridden by those of power, might, and position. Hence latently, though he may find expression in overactivity, we find the entity feel himself a little bit beneath that he attempts to gain.

The name then was Jeurepth. (2460-1)

Chapter 7

Abraham, Isaac, and Jacob

According to the Cayce readings, Melchizedek (Genesis 14) is the next appearance of the soul who had been Adam and Enoch—the soul who had chosen as his path of destiny to be the leader and savior of mankind, and later fulfilled it as Jesus, when he became the Christ.

In John 8:56–58, when the Jews were questioning Jesus, he responded, "Your father Abraham rejoiced to see my day; and he saw it and was glad." Jesus also told them, "Truly, truly, I say to you, Before Abraham was, I am."

If Jesus is harkening back to his experience as Melchizedek here, then Genesis 14 records, in a few brief lines, one of the most significant meetings of all mankind.

> *And Melchizedek brought out bread and wine; and he was the priest of the most high God.*
> *And he blessed him, and said, Blessed be Abram of the most high God, possessor of heaven and earth.*
> *And blessed be the most high God, which hath delivered thine enemies into thy hand. (Genesis 14:18–20)*

Abram not only rejoiced to see the "day" of this high priest, but also paid tithes. Abram was able to recognize the Living God manifesting in Melchizedek.

103

He had the same insight, apparently, that Peter did at a later date!

> *Jesus said to them, "Who do you say that I am?"*
> *Simon Peter answered, saying, "You are the Christ, the Son of the Living God." (Matthew 16:15–16)*

With all the nations, after Babel, turning to gratification and power, it became necessary for a new nation to be raised. Abram is the father of this people, a new nation dedicated exclusively to being *God's People*.

> . . . or as in the priest of Salem in the days when the call came that a peculiar peoples would proclaim His name . . . (364-8)

This nation was to be used for the renewing of the mind of man, restoring his memory through spiritual discernment.

> . . . a peculiar people, set aside for a purpose—as a channel through which there might be the discerning of the spirit made manifest in flesh. (2879-1)
> Thinkest thou that the grain of corn has forgotten what manner of expression it has given? Think thou that ANY of the influences in nature that you see about you—the acorn, the oak, the elm, or the vine or ANYthing—has forgotten . . . ? *Only man forgets!* And it is only in His mercy that such was brought about. For what was the first cause? Knowledge—knowledge! What then is that cut off in the beginnings of the Sons of God? Becoming entangled with the daughters of men, and the Daughters of God becoming entangled with the sons of men! As in Adam, they forgot what manner of men they were! Only as he lives, [as] he manifests that life that *is* the expression of the divine, may man *begin* to know WHO, where, what and when he was! (294-189)

Peter and Abram share several features in common, and reflect a universal spiritual pattern.

As a result of their spiritual development, both men had their names changed: Peter to Simon, and Abram to Abraham.

Their spiritual perceptions established them as the first patriarchs, or fathers, of their "church."

Peter's realization of the Christ in Jesus established him (or the awareness itself) as the "rock" of the New Testament church.* Perhaps Melchizedek bestowed a similiar blessing on Abram. Abram's awareness was the foundation upon which the Old Testament was built.

The discernment of the Spirit manifesting in the flesh is the base, or cornerstone, for this spiritual movement which began after Babel and the dividing of the nations, the foundation succeeding generations could return to and enlarge upon, building an ever-expanding body of souls attracted to each other for a common purpose.

> . . . for as given of Old, no soul can say that Christ is come of God *save* the Holy Spirit convict him of that statement. (262–72)

Just as Abram was able to see Melchizedek as the Son of a Living God, Melchizedek was able to recognize in Abram the elements of spirituality and worldliness that would establish him as the leader of this new movement.

In the following Cayce puts forth a simple, far reaching concept which in its application can be a working principle for all.

> Nations were set up then in various portions of the land [after Babel], and . . . set about to seek their gratifications. Very few—yea, as ye will recall, it even became necessary that from one of these groups

---

*See 262–87 A3.

one individual, a man, be called. His ways were changed. His name was changed.

Did it take sin away from the man, or was it only using that within the individual heart and purpose and desire even then, as man throughout the periods of unfoldment put—in his interpretation—that of material success first? (3976-29)

Abram's desire for material success was a principal motivation, but he had the willingness and the wisdom to let the Spirit direct him in the fulfillment of his ambitions.

Perhaps Melchizedek tutored him in this awareness and coached him in harmonizing his material desires with their spiritual source.

The earlier chapters of Genesis have been symbolic accounts of the Adamic race as a whole. With Abram, the book begins to focus exclusively on the development and history of a particular people.

Yet this people remain a symbol of mankind. As a struggling, seeking, oft-cursed, oft-blessed race, they are a microcosm of Humanity in its search for God, manifesting all the potential within for good and evil.

Melchizedek

These become hard at times for the individual to visualize; that the mental and soul [bodies] may manifest without a physical vehicle. (987-4)

Perhaps one reason why Melchizedek was able to impress Abram was that this high priest, like Adam and Enoch (and many of the so-called Eastern masters today) was a "living soul." Melchizedek was not a flesh man.

It is written of him:

Neither his father nor his mother is recorded in the genealogies; and neither the beginning of his days nor the end of his life. (Hebrews 7:3)

Thus, he was "a living soul."

For as He hath given, "The earth, the heavens will pass away, but my words shall NOT pass away." Know that the soul, the psychic forces of an entity, any entity, any body, are . . . eternal—for they are without days, without years, without numbers . . . (1376–1)

Cayce described the three primary appearances of Jesus—Adam, Enoch, and Melchizedek—as "in the perfection" (5749–14) and distinguished them from the later ones which were "in the earth"—Joseph, Joshua, Jeshua, and Jesus.

It is also written of Melchizedek that "he is a priest forever." (Psalm 110:4, Hebrews 7:17)

In his resurrected body Jesus is "without days or years" and once again High Priest "after the order of Melchizedek."

Though He were the Son, know that there was the lonesomeness, the fear of those influences that beset those He loved. Yet, knowing He hath entered into that glory, becoming the high priest of *His* people, they that seek Him daily, and having sat down on the right hand of the Father, then through Him ye have that promise, "Lo, I am WITH thee." (601–6)

The Offices of High Priest

Just as Abram began the line which eventually resulted in the ultimate incarnation in the flesh of the Son of the Living God, Edgar Cayce told a woman that in a very distant and ancient age, she had begun activities and established a line which made the appearance of Melchizedek possible.

Although Melchizedek's genealogy is not known, Edgar Cayce said that in prehistoric Egypt [884] had been his great-great-grandmother.

... we find the entity was in what is now known as the Egyptian land, during those experiences when there were those being sent as the emissaries for the peoples in the various lands; where there had been and were the attempts to correlate the teachings of those in various portions of that eastern land.

The entity was among those that aided in the establishing of that in the Persian land, which later became as the tenets of that people from whom— many ages later—Melchizedek came. And the entity finds that when this is said within its inner self there is a response which makes for an opening of the greater promises from within: M-e-l-c-h-i-z-e-d-e-k, the great-great-grandson of the entity, who came as without days, as without father or mother, yet as in [the] desire of the entity that—as Sususus—created or begun the condition through its efforts.

For it brought into the associations of those with whom the entity labored that which would make for peace, harmony; glorying in the acceptance of the truths from the Infinite—as it may express itself in the finite minds of men. (884-1)

If Cayce is correct, one of Melchizedek's greatest contributions to the spiritual development of mankind was the creation of the Book of Job, a religious allegory, a pattern of man's experience in the earth:

Q-4 Was Jesus, the Christ, ever Job in the physical body? ...
A-4 No. Not ever in the physical body ... For, as the Sons of God came together to reason, as recorded in Job, *who* recorded same? The Son of Man! Melchizedek wrote Job! (262-55)

Another body of teaching initiated by Melchizedek was later used to found the School of Prophets, which eventually became the Essene Community to which many of the early Christian Jews belonged, including Mary, Joseph, and Jesus.

Hence the group we refer to . . . as the Essenes . . . was the outgrowth of the periods of preparations from the teachings of Melchizedek, as propagated by Elijah and Elisha and Samuel. (254-109)

Thus the teachings of Melchizedek are not only the basis for much of the Old Testament wisdom, but the Christian philosophy as well.

Melchizedek's blessing of Abram in Genesis 14 provides another example of a spiritual service.

. . . Melchizedek, a prince of peace, one seeking ever to be able to bless those in their judgments who have sought to become channels for a helpful influence without any seeking for material gain or mental or material glory . . . (2072-4)

Father Abraham

Abraham, Isaac, and Jacob were the first patriarchs and set the examples. All the later prophets, seers, and writers of the Old Testament refer to the experiences of these three men.

God *spoke* to Adam, *walked* with Enoch, and *talked* with Noah, but only with the coming of Abraham, Isaac, and Jacob did man's concept of God become a personal thing.

On February 19, 1939, a fifty-four-year-old beauty salon manager obtained a Life Reading. In this very touching extract from it, Cayce describes the influence Abraham and his family had upon her.

. . . the entity was in that land when there were those activities in which the chosen of the Lord, as recorded, were making for those activities which later brought about the dwellings of him called father of the faithful.

The entity then was among the daughters of Heth from whom Abraham purchased the land near Socoh. [Genesis 23] The entity was acquainted with that patriarch, though—as considered in those days—of an unknown people; yet through the activities viewed by the entity as to same there was aroused that which brought a longing for a knowledge of a something of which the entity had heard.

For the manner in which Abraham, Isaac, and Sarah—and even Ishmael—were in the care of their own brought the love of a home; yet to the entity— as in the present—seeking rather the knowledge of that city not built with hands, but rather that eternal in the heart and soul of those.*

Hence we find again those abilities of ministering, of teaching—not as proclaiming but in LIVING, and in the quietness of the conversation, being able to give that which awakens within the minds and hearts of others that search for that which the entity finds in its emblem—the lamb *and* the lotus, in purity that touches even to the lips of God. (1825-1)

On May 2, 1935, a young writer was told of an early life and Abraham's effect upon her.

. . . when there were the settlings of the land, when first the land of promise came to be a portion of

---

*Revelation 21: ". . . there is then the new Jerusalem." For as has been given, the place is not as a place alone but as a condition, as an experience of the soul. Jerusalem has figuratively, symbolically meant the holy place, the holy city . . . the ark of the covenant in the minds, hearts, the understandings, the comprehensions of those who have put away the earthly desires and become as the NEW purposes in their experience, become the new Jerusalem, the new undertakings, the new desires. (281-37)

Abraham's or Abram's and Sarai's activity. The entity was then among the daughters of Heth, of those peoples in that land, in the name then Beloi, and was very closely associated with Sarah, Abraham, Lot, and those people that settled in those plains of Abraham. And the entity's daughter became then the leading among those that made for the combinations of the peoples of Isaac's son and those of the Canaanite land.

In the experience the entity gained, for it *proclaimed* many of those tenets or lessons or philosophies, or activities—as would be called in the present—as to establishing the relationships with individuals, and what became as the Creative Forces or that philosophy of life as pertaining to the Creative Energies as given out by Abraham during the period. The entity proclaimed same to the peoples roundabout, and made for the closer companionships with those first leaders of those people set apart for an activity in the earth. (846-2)

A Jewish businessman was told when Abraham went out from Ur, he had accompanied him. A love of travel and adventure is a result of that experience.

... before this we find in the promised land to those peoples who came up from Ur, and the entity was among those who served that leader, ruler, or patriarch, and gave much and required much at the hand of those about the entity in that day. Then the name was Shouel, and the urge as is seen—the desire of travel, and the urge of profit in traffic, for this, as is seen, is the greater influence in the present experience in earth's sojourn. (2855-1)

A twenty-year-old stenographer was told that Abraham had had a decided influence upon her in an earlier incarnation as one of his grandchildren.

. . . the early portion of those activities with Abraham, known as the father of the faithful. And the entity then was acquainted with those activities, being the daughter of Ishmael—Temah by name. And, being associated and acquainted with those activities and influences, the entity was among those who brought many of the changes in the affairs and activities of the peoples during that experience.

The entity held to rather the tenets of Abraham, as well as the knowledge of the activities of Isaac. (1709–3)

These readings spoke of the influence of Abraham upon others. The following suggests an influence which may have strengthened Abraham himself—*his mother!*

On January 30, 1930, a fifty-three-year-old housewife, a Theosophist, was told that following a life in Egypt, in 12,500 B.C., she had incarnated in India.

The entity then was among those when there came the destruction of the peoples in the valleys by those who *would* make rule from the hills. The entity then [was] among those who were *conquered* in body, but not in mind—and little by little the entity, through that experience, brings to bear such influence, such a condition, as to bring the peoples who would become the rulers in accord with the mental and the spiritual *builders* of that land, and of the house came Abraham. In the name Terahe. *Not* the father, but the mother. (115–1)

Abimilech

On October 18, 1934, a thirty-four-year-old physicist of Christian background was told he had been Abimilech, whose story is recorded in Genesis 20.

The entity then was in the name Abimilech, or the ruler of those people in the lands that lay between the

112

Egyptian and Syrophoenician lands. The entity then gained, even through those experiences and associations. Yet from those very activities there were brought those desires on the part of the entity, Abimilech, to bring to the knowledge of those who were as servants —or those whom the entity served in the capacity of the king of that land—that "he that would be the greatest among all would be the servant of all." While the entity had much in its experience and through that sojourn, that in the material and the moral life in the present would be questioned, yet the purposes, the aims, the desires, the activities were rather as the growth throughout that sojourn.

And the abilities of the entity in the present to apply same are in the innate influences that impel and make for a growth in the *soul*, or in the *entity*—which is the combination of all its experiences with its soul also—that may make for not only the material but the mental and spiritual growth that comes to a greater and better knowledge, understanding, of those things in the earth. (699–1)

As the above reading affirms, Abimilech was a spiritually-minded man. (Genesis 20) Unlike Pharaoh, who was awakened only through a series of plagues (Genesis 12), Abimilech was warned through a vision of the deception which Abram had practiced on him.

Abram's presenting Sarah as his sister previously in Egypt had not only protected them, but had established him, via Pharaoh's gifts, as a wealthy man.

Perhaps he and Sarah agreed to practice this deception everywhere they stopped, or when they felt it was needed.

. . . as indicated in the law of the Book, the life of the man Abraham was not beautiful, yet that faith which motivated same is beautiful, and the memory and of the children of faith we find beautiful. (4035–1)

Edgar Cayce's Bible class lesson was a hard look at Abraham and his rationalizations to Abimilech.

"Abraham's excuse was he did not feel God was in that place or among the people. He had become so used to thinking of himself as being a chosen one, he forgot to look for the good in others. He depended, rather, upon his ability for slyness and trickery.

"Abraham's actions, first with Pharaoh and then with Abimilech, are hard for us to understand. We can only say that he was very human. Even today, no matter how old we are or what our circumstances may be, we are constantly attempting to justify ourselves. Usually we are looking for the easiest ways to 'get by.'

"We might even say Abraham was just practicing another good Jewish trick, and getting a lot of money out of these people. The Philistines were as wealthy as the Egyptians.

"Still, if we think of the experience as something we can apply in our own lives, it would represent our attempts to justify ourselves in material things.

"Abraham felt he had a special interest in God not shared by others. Many feel that way today. They feel they are especially gifted and have a right to the best of everything. This is true. Each individual has a right to be best in life, but only in harmonious co-operation with others, and not at their expense.

"Abimilech reproved Sarah for taking his gifts to Abraham. He felt they were not deserved because they had taken advantage of him."

A Forced Issue

Even though Peter was able to recognize the Christ and was established as the head of the new Church, it became necessary, a very short while later, for Jesus to rebuke him. (Matthew 16:22–23)

The falling in and out of attunement is found in even the greatest ones in Scripture. They represent humanity in all its phases. And Abraham is no exception.

For remember, though he walked in many ways contrary to God's edicts and laws, Abram's try was counted to him for righteousness. (3129-1)

On October 18, 1941, a fifty-six-year-old missionary nurse was told in her Life Reading that she was a witness to one of Abraham's contrary ways.

. . . the entity was in the land of Pr, when there were those journeys of that one called. The entity was among those of that household, who knew and understood, and who made administrations for the welfare of Abraham and Sarah. The entity knew of those choices when there were the attempts on the part of man to force an issue with God. How oft ye find in thy experiences today that there are those same attempts on the part of individuals to tell God how they desire health, position, to be well spoken of. (2608-1)

In Genesis 15, Abraham, at ninety-seven, is told by God he would have a natural heir, a son.

In Genesis 16 Sarah, who had been barren all her life, urges Abraham to conceive the promised heir through Hagar, her personal slave.

"This," Edgar Cayce remarked, "was another instance where woman tempted man to try some other way than the one outlined by God. And Abraham, although called 'Father of the Faithful,' was willing to listen. Sarah was anxious. She wanted Abraham to receive the blessing which had been promised. So, she decided to help things get started."

"This is the way we are," Cayce continued. "If we plant a seed today, we dig it up tomorrow to see how it is growing. Patience is the greatest lesson—to wait upon the Lord."

As soon as Hagar conceived, she looked with contempt on Sarah. And Sarah become disturbed and angry.

The seed which had been planted bore its own fruit —this is the first instance in Scripture of jealousy and hatred between two women.

Cayce concluded the Bible lesson with the thought:

Sarah, no doubt, realized she had sinned, and for that reason, took it out on Hagar. Most of us will try and blame someone else, when we really know within ourselves that we are at fault.

Fearful of Sarah, Hagar fled into the wilderness.

In a psychic experience in the desert, she was told by an angel that her child would be ". . . a wild ass of a man, his hand against every man and every man's hand against him."

This child was Ishmael, from whom the Arab nations trace their descent.

Isaac and Ishmael

On October 16, 1940, Edgar Cayce used the following illutrations in a psychic discourse on the endocrine system of the human body.

When Abraham and Sarah were given the promise of an heir through which the nations of the earth would be blessed, there were many years of preparation of these individuals, of the physical, mental, and spiritual natures. Again and again it is indicated as to how they each in their material concept (watch the words here, please, if you would understand) attempted to offer a plan, or way, through which this material blessing from a spiritual source might be made manifest.

Hence we find as to how the material or mental self—misunderstanding, misconstruing the spiritual promises—offered or EFFECTED channels through which quite a different individual entity was made manifest; and through same brought confusion, distress, disturbance one to another in the material manifestations. (281-48)

It was Sarah's impatience in waiting for the fulfilling of God's promise which resulted in Ishmael's birth. When her spiritual development matured, the promise was fulfilled. Isaac was conceived!

Yet, when the last promise was given, that even in their old age there would be given an heir, we find that when Sarah thus conceived there was the development of a body physically, mentally, and spiritually so well-balanced as to be almost etheric in his relationships to the world about him, when the material manifestation had grown to maturity.

Here we find, then, that mind and matter are coordinated into bringing a channel for spiritual activity that is not exceeded in any of the characters depicted in Holy Writ.

When, then, were the characteristics, the activity of the glandular system as related to that individual entity? We find that there was a perfect coordination in and through the whole period of gestation, and the fulfilling of the time according to the law set in motion by the divine influence that was the directing force of both parents through the period.

We find also that throughout the period of gestation the activities about the entity, the mother, were such as to INFLUENCE the entity yet unborn, in patience to a degree not manifested in any other of the patriarchs. While the physical conditions made manifest in the body during the growth into manhood

117

were affected by MATERIAL laws, there was not the
changing or deviating whatsoever from the spiritual
through the mental.

Hence we find that illustration of what may be
termed the individual ideally conceived, ideally
cherished and nourished through the periods of
gestation . . .

What, then, were the developments of that ideally
conceived entity as related to the study here of the
endocrine system?

First, the individual was one conceived in promise;
with the desire, the purpose, the hope—in the act OF
conception—to bring forth that which had BEEN
promised. Hence the ideal attitude of both parents
in that individual case.

Hence as given, first the pineal, the cranial, the
thymus . . . then the gradual development of those
influences which brought a goodly child; one subject
to the care of both parents—by natural tendencies
from conception; bringing into materialization that one
worthy of being accepted and of RECEIVING the
promise beyond MANY of those who were of the
seed of Abraham. (281–48)

With the birth of Isaac, Sarah ordered Hagar and
Ishmael's banishment.

The Bible class notes offer some interesting and per-
ceptive commentary:

We wonder how Sarah could have been so cruel.
She had been the one who had brought Abraham and
Hagar together. However, this is a good lesson in
human nature. Usually when we obtain something
which is for us perfection, we want to rid ourselves of
everything that reminds us of imperfection.

Ishmael was a constant reminder to Sarah of her
lack of faith in God. She wasn't big enough to meet

her own sin, and bring up Isaac at the same time. No doubt this is why God favored the banishment of Hagar and Ishmael. He knew what each person was capable of accomplishing, and that they would have to work out their shortcomings together at another time. Everybody has to meet his own self eventually. The most important thing then was to create the proper environment for Isaac, who was to mean so much to the world. If Hagar and Ishmael had remained, perhaps it could not have been done.

Abraham and Edgar Cayce

The past and the present combine in this experience. On February 12, 1932, Edgar Cayce had the following dream:

"I thought I was with Mr. and Mrs. Lot and their two daughters running out of Sodom when it was raining fire and brimstone. What had been called, "She turned to a pillar of salt" (Genesis 19:26), because she looked back, was that they really passed through the heat which came from the fire of heaven, and all were tried as by fire. I got through the fire."

On April 1, a reading was given to interpret the dream. The reading stated that Edgar Cayce actually had been one of the messengers (Genesis 19:1, 15, 16) who had been sent to warn Lot and the citizens of Sodom. Evidently Edgar Cayce was one of the three who had spoken to Abraham beforehand. (Genesis 18)

In this particular vision, this is rather as an experience through which the body passed with those at the period; for the body then, the entity, was one that accompanied these bodies in this experience, and in the present must and will pass through—in the mental attitudes that are being assumed as respecting the body and activities—much as those bodies in that experience. As to whether [Cayce] is to remain in that of the escape, as then, or is warned as respecting the outcome of the individuals seen, depends upon the attitude and activities in the physical of the body through these trials; for they [the trials] will be as of by fire.* (294-136)

On April 2, the following day, a subsequent reading was given to interpret the above references. Although the dream related to a past life experience, it was attempting to communicate a message about the present. Edgar Cayce felt the dream pertained to the apparent necessity of leaving Virginia Beach, the place where previous readings had indicated he should settle.

After financial support was withdrawn from the Cayce Hospital and it closed at the onset of the Depression, Cayce faced a severe dilemma. Three homes into which he had moved were sold, necessitating further moves. Then he was unable to find a place to live.

In that as given of Lot, there was the choice by Lot as to whether this experience would be among the peoples in the city or those of the plains, or of those of the hills. The life was chosen rather among those, and companionship of these, of the city, which—in common parlance—"turned out bad!"

In the correlating with the life of Edgar Cayce, Virginia Beach was chosen rather by those sources through whom the information comes; and while the experience is as the attempt on the part of individuals and a group to make same so unpleasant as to cause much the same attitude as was forced to and through the life of Lot—but Lot's experience was besought by

*1 Corinthians 3:15.

a just man—Lot sought little for himself, save as to the gratifying of that as had been builded about same. So, as correlating the experience, then, of the leader or director at the time, and the experience as is in action of the *physical* manifestation of the body, rely rather upon those sources or channels through which such information and direction has come.

Believest thou that thou has contacted, do contact, those sources from which good may come to self or to others? Then *act* in that way and manner, irrespective of the attitude or actions of others. (294-137)

This reading expresses some of the pressures and problems confronting Edgar Cayce, but also gives us a rare view of the nature and character of Lot.

It is noted Lot sought little for himself, except gratification. Understanding this self-indulgent strain in an otherwise godly man gives us the basis for a possible interpretation of his daughters' incestuous actions (Genesis 19:31–35). If he didn't have it within him, they could not have seduced him.

"After his escape from Sodom, Lot refused to go with the angel to the mountaintop," Edgar Cayce commented and observed, "The mountaintop represents the place where man communes with God—or, where self must be met and seen in light of the Divine. Evidently Lot was not prepared to do this. He had been saved because of the prayers of Abraham, but even Abraham's prayers could not keep Lot from having to meet himself." Lot chose rather to go to "a little city" (Genesis 19:20), perhaps to commit his same follies, but in a "smaller" way.

Evidently Lot's wife shared the same weakness as her husband, as this reading indicates.

As the trust, the hope, the faith is manifested by the patience day by day, does there become the more awareness in self's own inner consciousness that all is well with Him; knowing that if the Lord is on thy side, who may be against you? Trust, and do that thou knowest to do, acting as the Spirit moves within— and look not back; remember Lot's wife. (262–25)

Q–1 In the reading of August 7, please explain what is meant by "Look not back; remember Lot's wife."
A–1 Looking to the front ever, for as one looks towards the light, the shadows fall behind and do not become stumbling blocks to individual development. Thoughts are things, and while the past that is passed may be used as stepping-stones to higher things, looking back causes one to stumble, even as Lot's wife looked upon that left as longing for those satisfying elements that made for the carnal, rather than the spiritual life. (262–28)

Abraham and the Power of Prayer

Edgar Cayce often referred to Abraham's intercession for Lot and the other citizens of Sodom and Gomorrah as demonstration of the power and potential of prayer. (Genesis 18:17–33)

As has been given, however, that which has prevented and does prevent the whole of civilization becoming a turmoil is the attempt of those who have the ideals of the Prince of Peace at *heart!* And as of old, the prayers of ten may save a city; the prayers of twenty-five may save a nation—as the prayers and activities of *one* may! But in union there is strength!
Then if that purpose would be kept, it must ever be kept in mind that we are our brother's keeper. (1598–2)

. . . where there were ten, even, many a city, many a nation has been kept from destruction. (3976–8)

The prayers of the righteous shall save many. "Where two or three are joined together in one purpose, I am in the midst of same." The combination, then, of both —for the supplication is putting self in that attunement to the forces as manifest in the growth, the development, of spiritual forces as are manifested in the material world. (136-45)

Why then the turmoil in the world today? They have forgotten God! Not that it is merely a karmic condition of a nation of a people; for know ye not that the prayer of one man saved a city? Think thou that the arm of God is shorter today than in the days of yore? (3976-25)

... even as Abram or Abraham—"If there be fifty, will it not be spared?" "O, if there be ten faithful, will it not be spared?" Then the hope of Europe depends upon *YOU* in your own home TODAY! In not the same way, but the same manner as did the life of Lot, or of the other peoples in Sodom and Gomorrah. [World Affairs Reading, January 15, 1932] (3976-8)

Though we may look upon, or feel that that which was given to Abram—as he viewed the cities of the plain and pleaded for the saving of same—was an allegorical story, or a beautiful tale to be told children— that it might bring fear into the hearts of those that would have their *own* way—may it not come into the hearts of those now, today, wilt *thou*, thine self, make of thine *own* heart an understanding that thou must answer for thine own brother, for thine own neighbor! And who is thine neighbor? He that lives next door, or he that lives on the other side of the world? He, rather, that is in *need* of understanding! He who has faltered; he who has fallen even by the way. *He* is thine neighbor, and thou must answer for him! (3976-8)

Abraham and Isaac: The Sacrifice

This lesson is taken from the Bible class notes:

"What is meant by God 'tempting' Abraham? In James 1:13 we are told, "Let no man say when he is tempted, I am tempted of God; for God cannot be tempted with evil, neither he tempteth any man. We understand from 1 Corinthians 10:13 that God does not ALLOW us to be tempted beyond our abilities, but with every temptation prepares a way of escape.

"The temptation, then, is not from God, but a result of a cause and effect law which has been set in motion. Our temptations come from our own deviations from spiritual laws in the past.

"In the case of Abraham, it would seem the sacrifice of Isaac was a supreme test, rather than a temptation. Yet it is impossible to conceive of God singling out one individual for testing or tempting, just to see what he will do. Certain opportunities were presented to Abraham as a result of natural cause and effect laws.

"When Isaac was born—almost a physical impossibility, considering their ages—it must have seemed a miracle to Abraham and Sarah. Abraham must have been throughly convinced of God's ability to do anything. His faith was so great he was willing to sacrifice Isaac, knowing God could and would restore him if his son was to be the channel through which all the nations of the earth would be blessed."

Good being from the all good, or as He gave there is none good save God—then that which would be good for an individual might not be to another godly; and thus it would be sin to that individual.

Thus Righteousness versus Sin becomes again a personal application of the individual's awareness of God's purpose.

For, as many be illustrated: to the workaday mind of today, Abram's offering of Isaac would appear foolish, yet—as stated—it was counted to him as righteousness, not sin.

This, then, is a personal application of the awareness that is in the consciousness of the seeker after God. (262-128)

In the symbolic, or metaphysical sense, the offering of Isaac, like the slaying of Abel, is a foreshadowing of the sacrifice of the Christ.

What, then, is this faith that is indicated? This one *knows,* when one becomes aware of same; yet may never put it into words nor tell another by words— or acts even—as to what that consciousness of faith is. Yet we may see the shadows of same in what faith has prompted in the experience of others, as it is so well expressed in the seventh of Hebrews, or as given in that God so had faith in man as to give His Son, HIMSELF, to die—IN the flesh; knowing that man must come to the realization—and would—that he, too, must often crucify that of material desire within himself, if he would glorify his better self, or if he would prefer his brother above himself. Or, even as a man, Abraham, the son of faith, the author of faith, offered —or was willing to offer—his only son, his physical heir; knowing that there MUST be a purpose from that inner voice as to that command. (2174-2)

The conclusion to this Bible class lesson is provoking and dramatic:

"Taking all the Biblical references regarding temptation into consideration, we must believe this was a very crucial period in the history of mankind. This was Satan's opportunity to deceive Abraham into destroying his own son, and thus thwart God's plan of salvation. Abraham's faith was so great in what he

125

believed to be God's command, Satan was thwarted instead. Through faith, Abraham was able to behold the other sacrifice.

"We can try and delude ourselves by saying there is no evil. If we believe in the record laid down for us, we must realize that Satan is abroad in the earth, seeking to add to his side all who listen to him. It is only those who have faith in God, as Abraham did, who can escape him.

"There comes a time of supreme testing to each soul—Abraham and Isaac, Jesus in the mount."

The Sons of Isaac

Sarah, Rebekah, and Rachel all had the same experience. They had to wait many years before they gave birth to their sons.

Other women were fruitful, and they were barren for most of their lives. Why was this? Were they not the chosen channels through which the line of Judah was established, and through which the Prince of Peace was eventually to come?

Those who are to fulfill the promises of God must first prepare themselves through patience, humility, prayer, and supplication. They must first become worthy to receive such a blessing.

Throughout history, the great spiritual leaders have come in answer to prayer and preparation, and through the need expressed by individuals and groups.

The Cayce information on ideals and purposes toward conception and sexual union are extremely significant in this day and time of world turmoil. Millions of people in the earth today seem to have no greater impetus than to fight one another, and to put selfishness and greed above love and service.

This is a continuation of the Edgar Cayce reading on the endocrine gland system, regarding the birth of twins to Isaac and Rebekah:

Then we have that illustration in the sons of Isaac, when there were those periods in which there was to be the fulfilling of the promise to Isaac and Rebekah. We find that their MINDS differed as to the nature or character of channel through which there would come this promise [Genesis 17:3–8]; when, as we understand, there must be the cooperation spiritually, mentally, in order for the physical result to be the same. HERE we find a different situation taking place at the time of conception, for BOTH attitudes found expression. Hence twins were found to be the result of this long preparation, and yet two minds, two opinions, two ideas, two ideals. Hence we find that HERE it became necessary that even the DIVINE indicate to the mother that channel which was to be the ruler or that one upon whom would be bestowed the rightful heritage through which the greater blessings were to be indicated to the world, to humanity, to mankind as a whole. [Genesis 25:23]

Hence we find two natures, two characteristics— physically, mentally, spiritually. Here we find what might be termed a perfect channel again and with same a testing—not only of the parents themselves but of the individuals that were begotten under those conditions in which the promise was as clear to them as it had been to Abraham. Here we find, as indicated, there was NOT a union of purpose in those periods of conception. Hence we find both characteristics, or both purposes of the individuals, were made materially manifest.

What then, ye may well ask, made this difference in the characteristics of the individuals; conceived of the same parents, under the environ or the law from the body of the one; with such a different characteristic made manifest as they grew to maturity?

As indicated, the first cause—that purpose with which the individuals performed the act for conception to take place, or under which it did take place. THAT is the First Cause! And the growth of that conceived under the same environ, through the same circulation, through the same impulse, was such that—when gestation was finished—one was of the nature or characteristic of the mother, the other was of the nature of indifference with the determination of the father; one smooth as the mother, the other hairy, red, as the father in maturity; and their characteristics made manifest were just those examples of the variations. Though conceived at once, born together, they were far separated in their purposes, their aims, their hopes; one holding to that which made body, mind, and soul coordinant; the other satisfying, gratifying the appetites of the physical and mental without coordinating same through its spiritual relationships to the progenitor or those conditions and environs from which they each drew their desires, their hopes, their wishes.

Do ye think that one received a different instruction from the other? Each received the same, yet their reaction, their choice of that in the environment made physical characteristics that varied in their activity.

Why were the characteristics such that one desired or loved the chase, the hunt, or the like, while the other chose rather the home, the mother, the environ about same? Were these depicted in the very physiognomy of each individual? When they had reached that period when the CHOICES were made, these were manifested. But when did they begin? What gland developed this characteristic in one and not in the other? The cranial and the thymus receiving the varied vibration, one brought harmony—not fear but harmony—with caution; the other brought just the opposite, by this "stepping up" in the rate of vibration. Or, if we were to study these by numbers, we would find one a three, the other a five, yet conceived together. . . .

Hence we find there the various forms of manners in which there is illustrated those characteristics that made for individual activity, that PROMPTED the carrying on of that through which the channel of hope might be made manifest. (281-48)

Another example regarding twins can be seen in the story of Tamar and Judah in Genesis 38.

Because Judah failed in his promise to secure a husband for his widowed daughter-in-law Tamar, she disguised herself as a harlot and sat at a roadside, waiting for Judah to pass.

Judah failed to recognize his daughter-in-law behind her disguise, and went in to her. The result of this union was a set of twins, one of whom became the ancestor of King David and, later, Jesus.

Is this a case of the two ideals at the time of conception finding expression?

Cayce states in the following Life Reading that Tamar's purposes were in keeping with God's will. Apparently Judah's were only for self-indulgence.

Before that we find the entity was in that now known as or called the Palestine land, during those days when the sons of Jacob sought for companions; and to one of the sons of Judah (Er) the entity, Tamar, became the companion.

Owing to the WILLFULNESS and the sin of Er, he was taken.* There was the command or the seeking that there be the fulfillment of the law of the day; and

*When this entity asked Cayce to describe the karmic relationship she had with her present father, Cayce responded, "He was Er, the husband in that experience. And is there a wonder that there are those disturbing forces in the material relationship in the present. Leave these with the Lord!" (1436-2)

Judah—in an unknown way—failing, yet the entity sought for that as would keep the issue of the body, and went in unto her own father-in-law; and bore two sons, one becoming then later the father of the fathers of Joseph and Mary—the parents of the Master.

There the entity was condemned, yes; yet her purposes, her desires were reckoned with by the God of mercy as being in keeping with His will and His ways.

Hence there is brought into the experience of the entity again the joys of knowing the Lord hath given, "Thy will, my will, are one with the Creative Forces."

And there is reckoned through the ages, then, that ye became as one that chose to do above the ways of men when the voice of man rose above thine own sex.

Hence in the experience, judgments are not taken away—if the entity will trust rather in the LORD than in the judgment of men, or the children of men.

For God is the same yesterday, today, tomorrow—yea, forever; and they that come unto Him in HUMBLENESS of heart, seeking to know His face and His way, may indeed find Him. (1436-2)

This Life Reading (1436-2) is one of the most interesting of all the Life Readings in the Cayce files.* In her next incarnation, Cayce states she was "the woman taken in adultery." (John 8:3-11) A remarkable similarity can be discerned in these two events when viewed in this connection.

Jacob's First-Born

The following extract is from a Life Reading in which a thirteen-year-old child was told that following an incarnation with Lamech (Genesis 4:19) he had been Reuben, the first-born child of Jacob and Leah.

*For an in-depth analysis, see Robert Wm. Krajenke, *Stand Like Stars* (Virginia Beach, Va.: A.R.E. Press).

Before that we find the entity was among the first-born of Jacob and Leah, and making for the expressions that in the beginning brought much that was in accord with the callings into an activity where these might have brought the blessings upon the activities in the sojourn. Yet when the desires of the flesh entered, and the associations with those things and about those peoples that had been as an expression of intolerance to those peoples, the entity made for the associations that brought disorder, discontent within those of its own household and those of its people in that experience and that expression.

These made for again those activities that have brought in the present the necessity of the awareness of the spiritual awakening within the expression and experience of the entity. (693-3)

As a youth, Reuben was a promising child. As he grew older, influences around him began to stimulate and awaken desires and emotions that were a portion of his former incarnation (from the time of Lamech). In Genesis 35:22, it is written he had sexual relationships with Bilhah, his father's concubine.

The deep affront that Jacob felt this to be is evidenced in Genesis 49, when the dying Jacob delivered his final words to his twelve sons. He cursed Reuben for defiling his bed, and prophesied he would never have preeminence. Reuben was "unstable as water."

Edgar Cayce's Life Reading for 693 shows how prophetic Jacob's words were. The record shows a pattern of deteriorating expressions throughout his incarnations. In the present life the child bore the heavy karmic burden of a severe form of epilepsy with multiple seizures, partial paralysis, and, in a broken home, was the bedridden dependent of a mother who did not want him.

Jacob labored seven years to wed Rachel, and was deceived by her father, Laban, who married him to his eldest daughter, Leah. Jacob contracted for another seven years and married Rachel. While Leah and his two concubines delivered ten sons, Rachel was barren. The long delay strengthened their love. When Rachel finally conceived, their first child was Joseph, the first *physical* incarnation of the soul who had been Adam, Enoch, and Melchizedek.

. . . the same soul-entity who in those periods of the strength and yet the weakness of Jacob in his love for Rachel was their first-born JOSEPH. (5023-2)

A child of Love! A child of love—the most hopeful of all experiences of any that may come into a material existence; and to some in the earth that most dreaded, that most feared. (5755-1)

The following discusses Joseph, and is a continuation of the discourse on the effects of the attitudes of parents on their unborn child. Apparently the superior attitude Joseph evidenced toward his brothers (Genesis 37) stemmed from the dominant mood of Rachel throughout her pregnancy.

Then, with Jacob and Rachel we have the material love, and those natures in which the characteristics of material love were thwarted. Yet in the very conception of same—though under stress (for there is held here by the mother the desire to outshine, as it might be poorly said)—we find a goodly child, one with all the attributes of the spiritual-minded individual; partaking of both the father and the mother in the seeking for a channel through which God might be manifested in the earth. And yet the entity had those physical attributes that brought into the experience of individuals those things that were reflected in the mind, in the movements and activities of the mother throughout the periods of gestation—when the entity had grown to manhood. (281–48)

The reading also describes the variation between Joseph and his younger brother Benjamin, and supplies the additional note that Benjamin was later Saul, first King of Israel. Reading 5148-2 indicates the same soul had also been Seth, the third child of Adam and Eve.

Also from the same attitude taken by those parents when the second son, Benjamin, was conceived— what were the varying characteristics here? The material love was just as great, the satisfying of material desire was completely fulfilled; yet it lacked that desire to BRING such as was wholly a channel through which the SPIRITUAL was to be made manifest. But it was a channel that EVENTUALLY brought the material made manifest in Saul, an incarnation of Benjamin. (281–48)

A Friend of Jacob's

Edgar Cayce's opening comments in reading 3851, a Life Reading for a thirty-eight-year-old Jewish interior decorator, were:

This is the fellow who fixed all the stakes for Jacob when he changed all the cows, you see, from spots and those that were roan. (3581–1)

The story which Cayce refers to is found in Genesis 30:25–43.

Before that the entity was in the Holy Land in the days when Jacob labored for the daughters of Laban, during those periods when the helpers of Laban chose rather to become helpers of Jacob.

The entity was among those who aided in preparing the places of feeding for the cattle when Laban had set up such and such conditions under which divisions would be made of the cattle or goods.

Thus those things having to do with wood, with blemishes, marks, spots, and things in wood are all of special interest to the entity. Today they may be called other names, but the entity finds that woods of gum and other solid woods that are known for their particular marking are of particular interest to the entity. And in themselves they carry a meaning that is not explained in the entity. But consider, such markings may even control the dispositions of people, as they did the animals. How truly the Lord is one, and moves in mysterious ways His wonders to perform among men. Ye say peculiar interpretations? But it's one.

The name then was Raoul. The entity journeyed to the Holy Land with Jacob. The entity was particularly interested in the happenings to Jacob when he wrestled with the angels. For the entity was one of those who looked after the son of Jacob when there was fear of the brother Esau, and remember there was only one of that particular group of sons in that particular period—Joseph. And the name means much to the entity in the present. (3581-1)

An intimation of a deep friendship is suggested in Cayce's response to the following question of 3581.

Q-2 What have been my past relationships and what are my present responsibilities with . . . Rosalyn?
A-2 In the Holy Land you were very close—yes, companions, and you were very close to Joseph, to Rachel, to Jacob. (3581-1)

The Only Daughter

Little is known of Dinah, Jacob's only daughter. Her story is told in Genesis 34. Historians dispute its authenticity as a historical fact. The story is viewed rather as an amalgam of many incidents, an allegory of the tribal warfare of that partiarchal age in which women were often defiled by invaders and revenged by their kin. Jewish scholars also question the historical validity of the Books of Ruth and Esther, suggesting they, too, are allegorical in nature.

However, the Edgar Cayce readings strongly suggest that in all three cases a historical interpretation is valid.

A twenty-four-year-old doctor's receptionist was told she had been Dinah in a previous existence.

. . . we find the entity was in the Promised Land, during those periods when there was the building of that which was and is a mighty influence in the relationships of man to Creative Forces.

There we find the entity was among the children of Jacob, and the daughter in that experience—one among twelve sons; and she whom Shechem sought, and over which much turmoil to Levi and Simeon was brought, owing to the conditions which arose through those activities as they journeyed in that land from the Arabian.

The entity gained and lost; and there are those experiences that arise accordingly in the present, from the activities in that sojourn—as to its relationships to individuals, owing to the social status, and owing to those conditions which arise in the activities.

Hold fast to that which is the purpose, and the promise. Remember, thou hast the promise within thine own self; and it is not as to who will descend to bring a message, or who would come from over the sea that ye might hear or know. For, Lo, He is within thine own heart, thine own consciousness. In thine own body has He promised to meet thee.

As ye have experienced the awareness of the arousing to healing, know that He IS life.*

Then the name was Dinah. (951–4)

Although Dinah is generally lost to history, the Edgar Cayce reading traced her progress both before and after her tumultuous experience as Dinah. In the previous life she had been in prehistoric Egypt, at the time of Ra-Ta, the high priest. She was one of his daughters, and served in the Temple Beautiful . . . "for the preservation of those activities in which there was to be rather the pure strain of the pure blood."

Cayce said she rose to power in the Temple Beautiful, but "united" with the influence of the Atlanteans "that brought the children of Belial's seeking for self-indulgences."

Her rape by Shechem and the bloody retribution by Simeon and Levi could possibly have been karmic in nature, a result of this Egyptian life.

Jacob's Ladder

The ancient ladder symbol which appears in this dream makes it particularly outstanding.

Q–11 [asked by Miss 993 in 281 series] Please interpret the following dream which I received a few days before Christmas: I was climbing a ladder and as I approached the top I became conscious of one round being out of the ladder at the top. It was with great difficulty that I continued to climb at this point. Thankful to say, I was able with my finger-tips to

*She had been healed of arthritis by following advice in her three previous readings.

reach the top. It took all my strength to pull my body up it. Those who were following back of me seemed to have no such difficulty, and one of the group made that remark. There was an answer by one already there, that as I made the climb I had laid the last round in the ladder.

A–11 Both prophetic and profound in this experience of the body-consciousness with the soul's experience. That the ladder represents the Way is evidenced, as has been given in interpretations for those that visioned even the ladder to heaven upon which there ascended and descended the angels of light. In that the rung was missing and that self had to make the effort to attain the top makes for those experiences oft in the mind's consciousness of many, that others that self considers as having an easy way do not become confronted with those hardships as is felt at times are experienced by others. But rather as the voice that came from above, when the self had made the way easier for those that would ascend by the experiences of self, that "I AM the way," knowing that He made of Himself no estate that others *through* Him might have access to the Father. And as the voice of those who cry the way is easier that thou hast made the last rung, for us; and as there is the cry from above, "Well done," there should come that peace within self that thine work of thine hand is acceptable in His sight. Be not unto vainglory, but rather in that happiness that passeth understanding in knowing that the work of thine hands is acceptable in His sight. (281–19)

Cayce again referred to the ladder when another woman, Mrs. 1158, requested a Life Reading:

As to the appearances in the earth, the one stands so far beyond the others—as indicated—that they become rather of little note; yet they each have their influence as a lesson, as a stepping stone upon the pathway. Or rather as that vision that was given of old—yea, which has been, which will become a vision to thine self—of that ladder upon which the rungs of life become here and there the pathway upon which the angels of mercy, light, patience, understanding, brotherly love, descend and rise again. As thou in thine experience has seen the ladder with the missing rung, know that such missing rungs are to be placed by not that as a service as duty alone; rather as the service of love, that ye may be even like Him. (1158-2)

The Promise to Jacob

In Genesis 32:24—28, Jacob wrestled with the angel, and was given the name of Israel. Later, on his deathbed, he prophesied to his son Judah that the scepter of Israel would not depart from his descendants.

Q-11 What should be understood by the statement [Genesis 49:10], "The scepter has not departed from Israel"?
A-11 Israel is the chosen of the Lord, and that His promise, His care, His love has not departed from those that seek to know His way, that seek to see His face, that would draw nigh unto Him. *This* is the meaning, this should be the understanding to all. Those that seek are Israel. Those that seek not, have ye not heard, "Think not to call thyselves the promise in Abraham. Know ye not that the Lord is able to raise up children of Abraham from the very stones?" So Abraham means call; so Israel means those who seek. How obtained the supplanter the name Israel? For he wrestled with the angel, and he was face to face with the seeking to know His way. So it is with us that are called and seek His Face; we are the Israel. Know, then, the scepter, the promise, the love, the

glory of the Lord has not departed from them that seek His face. (262-28*)

*The concepts of this reading are discussed in Robert Wm. Krajenke, *The Call to Israel* (Virginia Beach, Va.: A.R.E. Press).

Chapter 8

Joseph: Forerunner of the Christ

Throughout the story of Joseph, the writer keeps emphasizing that God was *with* Joseph. However, it was the God *in* Joseph which did the works. His great ability at dream interpretation was simply the natural expression of the Divine Within going out to meet the needs and circumstances of the moment. God is in all and "with" everyone who seeks to do His bidding.

Joseph is the first *physical,* or flesh, incarnation of the soul who had been Adam, Enoch, and Melchizedek—three experiences which Cayce described as "in the perfection" (5749-14).

Why, when he was a "living soul" with mind and Spirit attuned to the Creator, did he enter into the chaos of the earth plane, taking on a body of emotions and physical drives and desires that could, would—and did—separate him from this Oneness?

As the Savior, it was necessary for him to undergo all the experiences of man.

. . . would that all would learn that He, the Christ Consciousness, is the Giver, the Maker, the Creator of the world and all that be therein! And ye are His, for ye are bought with a price, even that of passing through flesh as thou, that He might experience and know all thy thoughts, thy fears, thy shortcomings, thy desires, the dictates of the physical consciousness, the longings of the physical body. Yet He is at the

141

right hand, *is* the right hand, *is* the intercessor for ye all. Hence thy destinies lie in Him. (696-3)

Cayce listed the life of Joseph as among the seven major incarnations of the Christ-consciousness in the development of the man Jesus.

The weaknesses of the flesh are evident in some aspects of Joseph's life. He inherited his mother's attitude of superiority. This is reflected in Joseph's relationships with his brothers. He expected them to be humble before him.

His ego also shows when, in Genesis 42, he accuses his brothers of being spies. He must have felt a bitterness and vindictiveness, and wanted to retaliate for some of the suffering they had caused him.

The divine is more apparent in Joseph than his weaknesses.

The following Life Readings show Joseph's influence on several entities and the spiritual awakenings this association created within them.

Truly do they show and anticipate Joseph's development as the Savior and Redeemer, able to bring all who follow Him back to their spiritual source.

An elderly Protestant woman, an authoress and lecturer, was told:

. . . the entity was in the Egyptian land, in that period when there were the preparations for the peoples of another land entering—or the days when Pharaoh of that period was aroused to activity by the voice of Joseph, the wanderer in that realm.

There we find the entity was among the daughters of that Pharaoh—in the name Kotapet.

In the experience the entity gained much through not only the mental application of those tenets of that messenger who came to save, as it were, a people as well as himself, but—as that entity was the messenger of the living God among those in a disturbed world —the entity caught that vision of the universal love as might be exemplified in the relationships of a people, of a nation—and not as in self-indulgence or self-aggrandizement for the passing appetites, or for those things that made for the laudation or the enslavement of any that material blessings might be in the experience of a few.

Hence we find again the entity giving of self in giving the expressions of mercy and grace among a people disturbed by those activities which had been as of a race consciousness in that sojourn.

In the present from the experiences in that sojourn, then, we find the great abilities in giving in word, in messages—that may be a part of the mental consciousness of the many—those things that will bring universal peace, universal love within the hearts and the realms of those who may take heed by the mental experience of this entity. (1837–1)

A middle-aged Christian Scientist was told she had been among the princesses of Egypt. Influenced by Joseph's teachings, she devoted herself to teaching the lower caste, or classes.

. . . the entity was in the land now known as the Egyptian, during those periods when there was the understanding gained by the ministrations and activities in the days when Joseph ruled in that land. The entity then was among the princesses of Egypt, and of that king who made for the establishing of that closer relationship to those who had chosen to serve the living God, rather than to serve their own selves.

For the entity was acquainted with and oft associated with Joseph, the incarnation of Him whom the entity later served so well in Thessalonica!*

---

*Her next incarnation in an early Christian community in Laodicea. See *Stand Like Stars,* (A.R.E. Press).

There the entity gained through the experiences in aiding those who were of the low degree or caste to become acquainted with the forces and powers that brought the greater comprehension and activities of the people in that sojourn.

Hence we will find in the present experience a lesson in the life of Joseph that is nowhere else gained in the writing of the Old Testament.

Then the entity was in the name Zerlva.

In the present application of self in respect to the lessons, the innate forces gained there, it is seen that there are the abilities to question with those who are seeking here and there for a greater comprehension of what the experience in materiality is all about—that which will give them, as then, an insight into the fact that it is the practice of the principle of patience that gives the development. For as He gave, "In patience ye become aware of your souls." (1825-1)

A follow-up reading for this entity supplies another page in Edgar Cayce's story of the Old Testament.

Mrs. Cayce: You will have before you the life existence in the earth plane of [1825] . . . and the earthly existence of this entity in Egypt as Zerlva, a princess of the king's household that established closer relationship to those who had chosen to serve the living God. You will also give a fuller explanation of the entity's experience there, and of her associations with Joseph and the knowledge of the truth and accomplishments gained there . . .

Mr. Cayce: In those periods when there had been the raising of Joseph from the keeper in the prison to a place of authority close to the king, then the entity—Zerlva—was a princess of the second wife of the King of Egypt in that period. His name is given here in the Exodus itself.

The entity in those periods was acquainted with the family of Joseph's wife; and thus became a worshiper of the one God.

After the famine and the restoration of the princess and the princes of Egypt, and the high priests of the various groups or cults, the entity then interested self in the activities of those peoples that sought gold and silver, and the gems that became a part of the regalia of the princess and prince of the Egyptian people, and that became a part of those things sought that were loaned to the children of Israel when they went out of Egypt. [Genesis 15:14; Exodus 3:21–22, 12:35–36]

This early period, though, was some several hundred years before this gold was turned to the Israelites by the Egyptians. But it was a portion of this same gold that was loaned to the children of Israel when they were led out.

The princess cared for those records that were kept for the peoples during that period, and became one loved not only by her own people but by the sages or older members of the household of the children of Israel. For it was the Israelites that the entity used for or entrusted with the activity of the mining of its holdings in the upper portion, or the southernmost portion of Egypt, in the hills and the mountains there. (1825–2)

The city of Heliopolis—or On—was a great Egyptian center of culture and learning. Joseph married the daughter of the high priest of this city, and thus was in a position to be exposed to and represent the very best in the arts and schooling of this flourishing civilization. This city later became known as Alexandria.

A teen-age Jewish girl was told in her reading that she had been the daughter of the high priest, and wife of Joseph.

. . . the entity was in the land now known as Egypt, when there were those turmoils that arose with those activities just before the periods of the famines in the land.

There the entity was that one whom Joseph chose as the companion, of all the peoples that were a part of his experience—the daughter of the high priest of Heliopolis.

Thus we find that the entity came under those tenets, those truths which were so much a part of her companion.

In the experience the entity gained throughout; in the abilities to make adjustments for the peoples of various beliefs, various activities—that brought peace and harmony throughout the sojourn in that land.

With the entrance of Joseph's father, the entity then —Asenath—studied what had been a part of the customs of the early patriarchs—Isaac, Abraham—who had been those who had brought such satisfaction, such an awareness.

Hence, as has been first indicated, the deep convictions of the spirit as may make alive in materiality are innate in this entity; and, with deep meditation, these may be aroused to mental AND material activity in the entity's relationship to others—as a helpful influence to all. (2444-1)

Everyone who came in contact with Joseph was influenced by him. With the arrival of Jacob in Egypt, carrying with him the legends and teachings of his ancestors, perhaps Pharaoh and others began to realize the real source of Joseph's abilities.

An elderly Protestant widow was told she had been in Pharaoh's household during the time of Joseph. The reading speaks of a new teaching, or understanding, introduced to the people.

. . . the entity was in the Egyptian land, during those

periods when there were those uprisings, when the activities and changes were wrought by the entrance and the raising of Joseph to position in the land.

The entity then was of the household of Pharaoh, who brought things to pass by the activities in that land. Thus we find the acquaintance with a new religious force, the new undertakings by peoples, and the variations between the spirit of an activity and the reality in physical manifestation (which is so seldom understood), or between the corporal and the spiritual.

In that experience the entity made manifest much of judgment, much of kindness, much of patience, and brought those activities that made for the greater expression, greater expansion, greater understanding through those trying periods of those peoples.

The name then was Tekla. The entity rose in authority and in power, and throughout the period of its experience in all the earth there were economic, social, religious developments for all those peoples.

In the present we find that power, might—by position, by association—should never be abused, but used to the glory of the Creative Force as prompted the entity through that experience. (2612–1)

The interpretations of the names of Joseph's two sons (Genesis 41:51–52) indicate how deeply he felt the suffering and outrage of his slavery and bondage. His anger is also shown in his accusation of his brothers as spies. Yet, as the following reading suggests, the deeper motivations in his relationships with his brothers was to return good for evil. Joseph tested his brothers. By concealing his identity and making all the trouble he did before revealing himself, his brothers had time to realize they were meeting their own sins. (Genesis 42:21)

The condition of the inner-man is reflected outwardly in weather patterns, climate changes, and other aspects of the environment. This concept, found in the Cayce

147

readings, is supported by many passages in the Bible. In the following, a suggestion is made that the seven years of famine were karmic in nature, a reflection of the sins of the people.

A Quaker teacher, and student of metaphysics, was told:

. . . the entity was in the Egyptian land, during that period when there were sore distresses being brought about by the sins of the peoples—and when Joseph was in the land.

There we find the entity was among the daughters of Pharaoh who ruled in that experience; coming in contact with Joseph and Joseph's interpretation of a living God.

This aroused in the experience of the entity, as Princess Teheru, the longing for a greater understanding, greater interpretation, as material blessings were shown. And the tendency for the entity to turn these into such became a stumbling block.

Yet, as there were those expressions of activities in which there were material blessings, there was love manifested. When there was given that understanding to the Princess as to how Joseph had made himself known to his brethren, and thus had asked Pharaoh— through the pleadings of the entity—that he might seek his father in his old age, and to his brethren give good for evil, there came another awakening to the entity in those experiences when there were such activities that the peoples brought those forces into the founding of what may indeed be called the Society of Magicians. This was founded, not for that purpose into which same has been turned, but by the offices of this entity.

Again, beware of that which holdeth not wholly to the spirit of the Christ, as it may be made manifest in the lives and hearts of men everywhere. (2067-1)

Joseph's abilities as a dream interpreter came through his attunement with the divine, or God within him. The other magicians attempted to decipher dreams through patient study of the known laws and rules. Because Joseph was attuned to the Highest, he was able to succeed when the others failed.

One entity was told he was one of the magicians in Pharaoh's court.

... the entity was in the Egyptian land, during those periods when there were the activities in which the land was ruled by an unknown entity—through unusual circumstances—which brought to the experience of the entity the unusual experiences.

For, the entity was among the magicians of Pharaoh's court during the period of Joseph's rise to power, and through those periods in which there was the consummation of the changing to the various conditions that arose in might and power through those periods. This brought that temperament, that tendency latent and manifested, for the questionings of powers, influences, and forces that direct human experience.

The name then was Tep-Lepan. The entity gained, the entity lost; gained during the periods of deeper thought and meditation, lost in the period of grudges, the period of attempt to apply necromancy as related to the magic, or the reasonings. (2386–1)

The Death of Joseph

And Joseph took an oath of the children of Israel, saying "God will surely visit you, and ye shall carry up my bones from hence."

So Joseph died, being an hundred and ten years old; and they embalmed him, and he was put in a coffin. (Genesis 50:25–26)

According to the Bible class lessons, Edgar Cayce believed Joseph had foreknowledge about his descen-

149

dants going into bondage. This premonition, Cayce said, may have been Joseph's reason for the oath, which requested his body be kept with them.

During the forty years in the wilderness, the children of Israel carried Joseph's body with them, although no mention is made of those who had the responsibility of caring for it. This was four centuries after Joseph's death.

If his kinsmen had taken his body to Canaan immediately after his death, as they did with Jacob, perhaps the Egyptians would not have allowed the Israelites back into Egypt to settle—and history might have been changed.

Apparently Joseph knew that his body would be a protection for his people.

Chapter 9

Exodus

From the time of Joseph until Moses there had been no noteworthy happenings to confirm the covenant which had been made with Abraham. The first chapters of Exodus, with background, details, and significant events in the early life of Moses, lead up to the renewal of the covenant. Through Moses God affirms the eternal contract He has made between Himself and His people —Humanity!

Not only is the covenant renewed through Moses, but it is enlarged upon, with the addition of definite rules, regulations, and laws which must be followed. New prophecies and promises are added. Many of the events throughout Exodus are the fulfillment of prophecies which have already been made.

As one through whom the covenant was being renewed, Moses had to become a "living" example of the power and presence of the God he worshipped. He not only had to receive and record the law, he also had to comprehend its significance and be able to interpret it for those he had to lead. In order to have this understanding, he had to live in accord with all that came through him as a divine channel.

In Egypt, as in every other country at that time the people worshipped idols, statues, and other physical objects which represented attributes and activities of their gods. For the Egyptian, the serpent was the god of wisdom. The bull represented strength. The hawk and the eagle governed mental superiority. Everything that was necessary for material existence was represented by some figure. They were worshipped by those Egyptians who were seeking to manifest the particular attributes or aspects embodied in that god.

When Moses approached Pharaoh and asked that his people be given their freedom to worship, Pharaoh wanted to know what their god was like. He assumed it would be represented in some definite, concrete material form.

Moses was challenged with the task of bringing the Hebrews, once again, into the realization that their God was a living God, one whom they could worship in spirit, and who would answer prayer.

In this crucial period in Israel's history, Moses established a new relationship between man and God. Before this, the people always worshipped the God of their fathers. The people never prayed, "Our God—My God," but always to the God of Abraham, Isaac, and Jacob.

Moses established a means by which God can be approached directly, and thus become more personal to each individual.

Edgar Cayce felt that the new identity of God as Jehovah was like a sign to the people. The name made Him more personal, just as the name Jesus does for the Christian. Throughout the Exodus, the Hebrews began to feel, experience, and comprehend the awareness of the presence of the divine in their lives. Jehovah became the most endearing word by which they could refer to this all-powerful, unseen, creative force manifesting through them. The covenant which had been made to Abraham, Isaac, and Jacob began to be more real to them.

This promise, Edgar Cayce said in one of his Bible class lectures, was renewed in Jesus, who said he would bring into remembrance ALL things, even from the foundations of the world. Just as it was necessary for the Hebrews then, he taught, it is the responsibility of

152

the individual today to make that promise real in his own life.

Joshua: An Aide to Moses

The first five books of the Bible are called the Torah by the Jews and represent the most significant portions of their Scripture. Although traditionally attributed to Moses, Edgar Cayce suggests that Joshua may have had a great responsibility in formulating these concepts.

Only by accepting the incarnations Cayce attributes to the development of Jesus do we have the basis for understanding the following:

> . . . from the very first of the Old Testament to the very last even of Revelation, He is not merely the subject of the book, He is the author in the greater part, having given to man the mind and the purpose for its having been put in print. (5322–1)

Adam entered the earth to be the savior. Enoch was a prophet, and, if the traditions and legends are accurate, dedicated himself to preserving records of the Law of One. Melchizedek wrote the Book of Job, and was the author of teachings used later by Samuel and Elijah in founding the School of Prophets.

Joseph initiated the first period of bounty and favor for Israel as a nation. After his death, the period he instituted gradually deteriorated into bondage and servitude. After the passage of four hundred years, this soul then reincarnated as Joshua and was instrumental in leading Israel out of Egypt into the Promised Land of Canaan, for the second material kingdom in their history.

Although "writings of Joseph" are mentioned once in the Cayce readings, nothing is known about them. Yet, they must have influenced, or have been assimilated into portions of our Scripture.

Two readings refer to Joshua as the "interpreter" and "mouthpiece" for Moses. Reading 364–5 states Genesis was compiled from existing, ancient records and from information obtained by Moses through deep meditation. Joshua no doubt aided Moses in understanding the meanings of the old manuscripts and interpreting those experiences while in altered states of consciousness. It is quite possible both Joshua and Moses were psychic and clairvoyant.

It is twice recorded that Joshua accompanied Moses when he went to commune with the Lord on the mountaintop (Exodus 24:13) and in the tabernacle (Exodus 33:7). Only Joshua was permitted to do this. Not even Aaron, Moses' own brother, was allowed to accompany Moses.

In the light of these possibilities, Joshua becomes one of the most outstanding and significant characters of the Old Testament.

The Birth of Moses

Four-hundred-year cycles play a recurrent part in the spiritual history of Israel. When the book of Exodus opens, the four-hundred-year period of captivity foretold to Abraham is nearly completed. Four centuries have passed between the death of Joseph and this soul's rebirth as Joshua. An identical time span occurs between his last Old Testament incarnation as Jeshua, the high priest at the time of the rebuilding of Jerusalem, and his birth as Jesus.

Throughout the later history of Israel, it will be seen that the prayers of the people in times of distress or servitude have resulted in the incarnation of a great leader. Moses is the first of these figures, and the one who dominates the entire Old Testament. Many other great leaders will follow, who always arise when the people have returned to dependency on God.

The details of Moses' birth and his being set adrift on the Nile, to be discovered by the princess, are a familiar story to all of us. However, in a reading for an Iowa housewife, who was told she had been a handmaiden to this princess, Cayce supplied additional facts. Note the touching detail about the lilies.

Before that, we find the entity was in the Egyptian land when there were those beginnings of the preparations for the coming of the lawgiver. The entity was among those of the maids to the princess of Egypt, and the individual who waded into the river to bring the little ark or bassinet ashore with the babe in same. About the babe were lilies, which is a portion of the symbol, and it is a gentle reminder of the law given by the entity [Moses] whom the servant or maid brought to this princess. These should be reminders and thus keeping the law. For the law of the Lord is perfect and it converts the soul as application is made in same through patience. The name then was Abatha. (5373-1)

The orthodox interpretation has always been that the child was immediately taken into the Egyptian court and raised as an Egyptian, with the child's mother hired as his nurse. Yet the following reading, given in 1944 for a woman from Pennsylvania, indicates the child was not raised as an Egyptian for the first several years, but in his own home, among his own people. Several members of the Egyptian household accompanied the child, and, like this maiden, were exposed to the spiritual influences in that home.

Before that, we find the entity was in the land when there were these who gathered about the ark which had been placed in the Nile. The entity was then a maid to Pharaoh's daughter and one who was given the privilege to be in the household of Moses' mother during the rearing of the babe who became the lawgiver to the world. For this is the basis of the activity. Thus the entity, in the name then Tanai, heard the prayers, not only of Jochabed, but Miriam, as this

155

entity saw the child grow and knew that for which it was destined, that there were those forces, those influences such that indeed the soul of each entity is a corpuscle in the body of God. (5367-1)

Another woman, a Christian service volunteer in her present life, was told she had been an instructor to Moses. The reading also suggests an exchange of ideas and information between the Egyptian teachers and the Hebrews.

Before that, the entity was in the Egyptian land, during that period when there were the preparations for those activities which brought about the return of the children of promise to the Promised Land.

The entity then was in the household of the Pharaoh, and in the name Tahi. The entity encouraged those activities and aided in the instruction of Moses as not merely an Egyptian but from the associations with Jochabed, the entity learned from the scribe Ezakiai [?] of those promises that had been made to the saints before Abraham, Isaac, and Jacob.

These became a part of the entity's experience. And when there were the journeyings from the Egyptian land, the entity was among those who went with Moses, Aaron, and Miriam; the entity being a close associate of Miriam through those periods of journeying, and strengthened the hands of those who aided in preparing the way. (2574-1)

The sympathy and understanding of many highly placed Egyptians is further evidenced in this extract:

Before that, the entity was in the earth during the period when there were those preparations for the journeying of the people of promise from the Egyptian land, in that period when the Pharaohs were in authority over that people.

The entity then was the daughter of Pharaoh, and a sister of Bithiah who nurtured and brought up Moses as her son. This daughter was not mentioned in Holy Writ, yet she wielded a power for good in those periods, even as did Bithiah.

The entity aided in changing the edicts by the influence it wielded over the overseers and the counselors to that Pharaoh; thus lightening, in a great extent, the burdens of those people. (2550-1)

Moses Slays an Egyptian

And it came to pass in those days, when Moses was grown up, that he went out among his brethren, and saw their oppression; and he saw an Egyptian beating a Hebrew, one of his brethren of the Children of Israel.

And he looked this way and that way, and when he saw that there was no man watching, he slew the Egyptian and hid him in the sand. (Exodus 2:11-12)

Using this episode as it is presented in the Bible, Cayce and his Bible students drew the following conclusions:

"According to Egyptian law, Moses should not have taken the Hebrew's side. This incident shows his sympathies were entirely with the Hebrews. Moses had a violent temper. This is indicated in many instances throughout his life.

"Although he was trying to help them, the Hebrews resented it and taunted Moses with their knowledge of the slaying. This is the attitude of many today who are in trouble and yet resent any interference.

"Who told Pharaoh about the slaying? It must have been one of the Hebrews, someone who had no more understanding of Moses' purposes than the one who disputed with him. To the Hebrews, Moses was an Egyptian. They did not know he was one of them, who wanted to help his people. Perhaps they thought it was a personal malice which prompted Moses to kill the taskmaster. He did it so quickly, in a fit of temper, the Hebrews never knew the real reason."

Just as Cayce suggested to his Bible class, perhaps the real reason for this murder has never been known or understood. The version we have in the Scripture is framed in such a way that it highlights Moses' love for and involvement with the Hebrews.

Yet a different story of this same incident is told in a Life Reading given for an attractive twenty-year-old woman:

Before this, we find the entity was in that period when many changes were brought to a people throughout the world.

The entity then was in that land now known as Egyptian, during the period when the princess Hatherpsut (the entity's mother) was in power; and the entity's name was Sidiptu, hence a sister of that leader Moses, the lawgiver of Israel.

During the reign of the mother, the entity was associated with those people later despised on account of the love (physical) that the mother found in association with a peoples.

And the entity was then pledged to one of the leaders of Israel, in the house of Levi; and being despoiled by an Egyptian, it was *this* one that the brother, Moses, slew, hence causing that disruption which brought—at the latter period of the mother's and the entity's sojourn in the land—a *new* pharaoh to the *ruling* of the peoples; this one coming then from the mountain or southern land of an almost divided land over this incident in the entity's experience.

While the entity may be said to have gained and lost, gained and lost through the experience, under the tutelage of those peoples with whom the brother was associated—as did the entity's mother—much un derstanding was brought of the legends of a people that had been called for a particular service.

This is noteworthy of interest, then, in the entity's experience in the present; that to the entity, one that has had an experience that deals with the universal manifestation of a spiritual or unseen power is sacred to the entity.

Hence another reason for precaution in self, as the developments come—and will come, if there will be the application of self in the mysteries of the unseen that may come for self.

And it is well that self, when contemplating and meditating, surround self with the environs of an oriental nature; for the dress itself should ever be rather the robes or loose clothing about the body. There should ever be something that is *old,* something that is plaid; something that bespeaks of either the scarab, bull, or serpent; with the perfumes of the East.

But know that these are but those things that will make for the arousing *of* the *inner* self, and *not* the force that *arises;* rather a *material* element for the *producing* of same.

And the abilities from the experience of the entity in Egypt may be brought forward in the present, in aiding to give much to peoples that seek for the development of self and of their relationships with the Creative Forces and their relationships to their fellow man.

For, the wisdom of Hatherpsut may be in the entity in the present experience as a *builder* in a mental, a commercial, or a material way.

The spirit of the mother in that experience, then, may *yet* aid and guide in the present; *beautiful* in body, *beautiful* in mind in the experience, yet turned the world upside down! (355–1)

The Edgar Cayce readings admonished many individuals to be either hot or cold—good or bad—but *be* and *do* something. God can work with desires and emotions, no matter at what level, as long as they are in action. But He cannot work with energies that have become static or lukewarm. (See Revelation 3:14–16.)

Although the anger that resulted in the taking of a life cannot be condoned, the necessity to flee took Moses to a place where there could be the further unfolding of his own consciousness, and of his destiny. The flight from Egypt took Moses to the land of Midian, where he married into the household of Reul, a priest of that land. (Exodus 2:15–22)

The Eastern sages have a saying that "when the pupil is ready, the teacher appears."

Reul is also called Jethro, an honorary title connected with his office as priest. Reul is also referred to as a prince of Midian, and the Midianites were descendants of Abraham. Jethro must have been well versed in the lore, legends, and teachings concerning Abraham. He no doubt was familiar with the prophecy in Genesis 15:12–15, concerning the years of bondage.

Now that this period was nearly over, we wonder how the priest interpreted the strange events which led an Egyptian prince of Hebrew blood to his tent. Perhaps Reul had already been prepared through dream or vision and recognized Moses as the channel through which the prophecy of deliverance would be fulfilled.

As a shepherd, alone in the midst of nature for long periods of time, Moses had ideal conditions in which to absorb the teachings of his father-in-law, and to meditate upon his destiny.

While his people in Egypt "groaned under their oppression" and began to build the desire to be free, Moses was preparing himself for the part he was to play.

The Burning Bush

The burning bush that appeared to Moses appeared in a vision to a member of Cayce's original Search for God group. The interpretation which Cayce gave to her can be applied equally as well to Moses:

Q-10 Please explain the experience I had on the morning of July 17, in which I saw a pyramid of smoke over my head and then a burning bush within. What do these symbols mean?

A-10 The awakening to that as must be a portion of the experience necessary for the full cleansing, the full awakening to the possibilities that lie within.

How hath He given that ye shall be purged? Even as by fire. This, to be sure, is emblematical; that thy service may rise as sweet incense from the altar of service in thyself. So long as ye look upon a service done, a good deed, as a lesson, as a duty, as a service, so long are ye subject to same.

When to do good is the joy, when to deny self is a pleasure, *then* thou wilt know the I AM is awakened within. (262–85)

Like this woman, Moses had to be brought to the point where there could be an awakening to the purposes for which he had entered into the earth, and to realize the "possibilities" within that would aid him in fulfilling that purpose. At the time of his vision, Moses was handicapped by fear and doubts. He felt unable to lead the people because they did not know him, and hindered as a spokesman because he was a stutterer. But as he applied himself, he outgrew his limitations and gradually became aware of the "I AM" within.

Perhaps Yahweh, or Jehovah, was such an endearing and an oft invoked name, because of the effect the sound vibrations had upon the conscious and subconscious minds.

It was the word which Moses heard during his experience of inner awakening. The combinations of the letters and the phonetic sound of a word, which Cayce suggested to one individual to stimulate an inner awakening, is very reminiscent of the "I AM THAT I AM," or JEHOVAH, heard by Moses—and carries the same significance!

Q–4 Give meaning and pronunciation of the word J-A-H-H-E-V-A-H-E.
A–4 Java; meaning the ability within itself to know itself to be itself and yet one with, or one apart from, the infinite; to be a part of that realm of helpers; to know self as a part of and in that realm where the angels are, or in that realm of the individuals who have been, who are, with the Announcer, the Lord of the Way, and who have attained the consciousness of the Christ-within. (2533–8)

A Discussion

The Bible records a dialogue between Moses and God:

And Moses said to the Lord, I beseech thee, O, My Lord, I am not eloquent, neither heretofore nor since thou hast spoken to thy servant; for I am a stutterer and slow of speech.

The Lord said to him, Who has made man's mouth? or who makes the dumb, or the deaf, or the seeing, or the blind? Is it not I, the Lord?

Now therefore go, and I will be with your mouth and teach what you shall speak.

And Moses said to him, O, My Lord, send I beseech thee, by the hand of whomsoever thou wilt send.

And the anger of the Lord kindled against Moses, and he said to him, Behold Aaron, your brother, the Levite. I know that he is a good speaker, and also behold, he will come forth to meet you, and when he sees you, he will be glad in his heart.

And you shall speak to him and put my words in his mouth; and I will be with your mouth and with

his mouth, and will teach you what you shall do.
(Exodus 4:10–15)

Actually, these issues, such as the power of God, Moses' limitations, and Aaron's usefulness, could have been debated by Moses and his kinsmen. The following was given to a middle-aged Lutheran minister.

Before that, we find the entity was in the land of the high hill, but much different than is presented by the name alone in the present. For the entity was among those who aided, studied, disputed with Moses when he had had his vision that he must return to Egypt for the relieving of the pressure upon the chosen people. Not because of any particular thing, save their desire, their search, their one ideal in the fact of a living God that might be touched with the infirmities of the human experience. (5159–2)

In another reading, Cayce says Moses was "slow to comprehend" (5276–1) the message of the burning bush. However, through the convictions brought about during that vision and from the understanding derived from study and debate with his kinsmen, Moses was ready to commit his purpose into action.

Willing as his spirit was, he applied it with misunderstanding.

When there had been fulfilled that preparation, or a part preparation of material knowledge of Moses, he set about to put into activity that purpose for which he had come into the earth. Yet materially he chose an error, a sin, in establishing the righteousness of his fellow men. Thus a full period was required—as of earthly righteousness or earthly knowledge—to undo or to coordinate that [which] was to be a working principle of righteousness versus sin. THEN he was

CALLED; as was Paul in his persecution of the church, conscious of a purpose but ACTIVE, DOING something TOWARD an activity which by education to him (physically) was correct, yet sin.

He, too, was called and directed. So, too, may each individual be active in principle, in purpose, being sincere, being direct. Thus may the individual gain the greater working knowledge of that which is righteous, versus that which is sin.

Then, let each be not slothful, not putting off, not unmindful that ye must be up and doing, working, BUSY at that which is to thee, NOW, TODAY, that as thy conscience directs thee to do; in sincere, direct manner. And ye may be sure He counts that try as righteousness; and the sin that may appear to self or to others is but upon the reverse—which is righteousness. (262–126)

Once we realize we have a purpose, or a "calling," we should not let fear or ignorance hold us back. If we begin to apply what we know we are supposed to do, guidance, direction, and further enlightenment will follow. Using Moses as an illustration, Cayce points to this spiritual law in the following:

Q–6 In what way may I best attain my ideal?
A–6 In the applying of self day by day in every way, that thou *knowest*, that makes a personal application of that thou knowest to do, without questioning of the morrow; for the *morrow* has *its* evils and its goods, sufficient unto self. Today is! Use that thou hast in hand. So does the awakening come. Even as called by God to lead a people, as was Moses, a shepherd, and the flocks in Moab. Use what thou hast in hand, for the *ground* whereon thou standest is holy! Do thou likewise! (262–13)

Perhaps, instead of establishing a concept of racial superiority, the more spiritually correct attitude would have been an expression of universal brotherhood in which no race or special group was favored, as is seen in the following:

Q. What should be the attitude of this country toward the refugee problem as it relates specifically to the Jewish people? Please explain their problems.
A. They are like every other individual. THEIR problems, so long as ALL are considered, is one. If they themselves become secular or become tyrannical in their nature, then this—too—will become a problem in America.

The attitude toward the refugees—they that entertain those who are without home, or hungry, may entertain the Lord himself. For "As ye do it unto the least, ye do it unto thy Maker." That should be the attitude, ever. But LIVE, each soul, in such a manner as to implant not the bigness of the individual but the love of God made manifest among men!

These are problems not only, then, of the Jewish peoples, but of those of every cult, or every "ism" or "cism." For remember the first principle—ALL are equal before God! (3976-24)

Pharaoh's Hard Heart

Oft will it be learned by the study of phenomena of a people's action, that seemingly all forces in the universe are used to bring about that which is good, for it has been said, "I will harden the heart of Pharaoh, that he will not let my children go." Through this same seed came the Son of Man, and through these same trials through which the forefathers passed, the burdens and sins of the world were laid upon the Son.

Then, through the trials, the temptations, the besetters of evil from within and from without, may any work that is His [God's] be expected to grow, and in that manner become polished bright, and a shining light unto the world. (254-31)

Why did God harden Pharaoh's heart? The power of a living God had to be impressed upon the minds of the people. Several hundred thousand people had to be convinced that the plagues and miracles conjured by Moses were not merely magician's tricks, but actually manifestations of God's power, and a result of Moses' attunement. The Egyptian magicians were students of metaphysical laws. Either through feats of materialization, or thought-control over the minds of others, they could make sticks turn into snakes, or have grains of sand change into lice or fleas. The magicians were versed in all the possibilities contained in the manipulation of three dimensional laws. Yet Moses and Aaron were able to go beyond these feats because they were attuned to an infinite source of Creative Energy.

A gifted leader is able to sway throngs of people to respond to great causes, but it takes faith in a spiritual ideal—not just a belief—for individuals to keep their attention and efforts consistently and persistently focused in one direction.

If the people believed Moses was merely a better magician than the Egyptians, there would not be sufficient devotion to carry them through the trials once they achieved their freedom. They had to believe that God was speaking through Moses, and that Moses was manifesting His power. Moses later tried to teach the people that they, too, could attune themselves to God and that He would speak to them. In essence, Moses was telling them that all the magic could be theirs if they would attune themselves to God and use it for His purposes.

Most of us are like these Hebrews, Cayce explained. Human nature does not change. We believe in God, but every time a hardship or difficulty arises, we falter in our beliefs.

Just as human nature stays the same, so do the magic and miracles of that period—we merely call it by other names. Today scientists are still working with three dimensional concepts and understanding. And what is it they discover? Just another way of using God's laws. Their discoveries may be used for the glorification of the Spirit in the earth, or result in the destruction of everything that is good, including the best that is within us.

Unless the Pharaoh's heart became "hardened," there never could have been built a great desire in the people to follow Moses. The increasing manifestations of the great power he was united with was essential in building that desire. All the things which happened then were necessary to raise the morale and consciousness of the people who had been slaves for several hundred years.

A teacher to Moses learned much as she watched the changes in the hearts and minds when Moses returned and set the people free.

In 1942, this entity was a widow, a nurse, and a student of Unity, but in the past . . .

. . . the entity was in the Egyptian land, when there were those peoples making preparation for the sojourning from there. The entity was among the children of those peoples who saw that activity; being then a maid to Pharaoh's daughter that discovered the babe, Moses, that saw the unfolding of that life in the varied environs, that heard much of the cries of those peoples as through those years their tasks were made harder and harder.

It may be said that the entity was a teacher, in a manner, to Moses; and thus the wisdom of old is of special interest to the entity. Ritualistic activities of mind and body to bring effects within same find a deep something within the entity.

The name then was Zeruba. The entity gained the greater in the mental and spiritual unfoldment in the experience, as it watched, as it meditated upon the happenings as the entity grew older and watched the unfoldment of those who were in authority and as these things changed in their relationship to the material happenings.

Thus lands, nations, various peoples, and their problems as peoples and individuals are of interest. Thus the entity is innately something of a historian, as well as mentally and manifestedly in mind. These abilities may be used to material advantage if the spiritual purposes are in keeping with that which is ever creative, as manifested in the Son. (2851-1)

How did Moses feel as he returned to Egypt? He had obtained a very high state of consciousness through his experiences in Midian, under Jethro's tutelage. Now the knowledge he obtained demanded application. This is a law the readings constantly pointed to—"Knowledge not applied is sin." Moses had foreknowledge of the slaying of the first-born, and knew he had to prophesy this to Pharaoh if he refused to release the Hebrews. Moses certainly believed in the divinity of his mission and the fact of God's protection, for what he was called to do was almost certain death under the laws of the state.

With his first confrontation with the Pharoah, Moses had every right to believe the prophecy about his heart was correct. Pharaoh reacted the way men who have held absolute power have done through the ages. His religion or philosophy made him the most important figure in the earth, and kin to the divinities of heaven. Pharaoh was not ready to change this concept for another which might alter his opinion of himself.

The Plagues

The basis for a later experience as a helper to Joan of Arc, Cayce told this young lady, is found in her life as an assistant to Moses and a witness to those many miraculous deeds.

Before that the entity was in the Egyptian land, when there were those preparations for the exodus; during those periods when the lawgiver was active in bringing the awareness or consciousness to the pharaohs of that period.

The entity then was of the household of that assistant to Moses—that is, of Aaron's household; not as a daughter or as a relative, but rather as a helper in that preparation needed for those periods of activity. Hence, as is experienced by the entity, there is latent within self a constant looking for divine or outside interference with activities of individuals or groups, and rarely does the entity look to same for itself. Yet know, as the lawgiver gave, it is within self. For, thy body is indeed the temple of the living God, and there He meets thee.

The name then was Ceclia. (2936-2)

Another reading tells us:

Magicians then were not merely sleight of hand performers, or prestidigitators, or those who worked mysteries, but rather they were—as would be termed today—the lawyers, or the students of laws of EVERY nature pertaining to the ruling and directing of the subjects of a kingdom or of a household. (2386-1)

Because the magicians of Egypt were versed in the arts of reproducing phenomena, they could easily duplicate Aaron's feat when he cast down his staff and it turned into a serpent. (Exodus 7:8-11) The Egyptians, as Edgar Cayce points out, were schooled in all magic— or laws—up to a certain point. But the ability—or attunement and purpose—of Moses and Aaron enabled them to transcend that level of material knowledge.

For they cast down every man his staff and they became serpents; *but Aaron's staff swallowed up their staffs.* (Exodus 7:12)

Perhaps it was a flash of intuition, or an inspired moment. There is a tradition, as Churchward points out,[*] that this confrontation was between the *minds* of Aaron and Moses and the priesthood. They were both schooled in occult sciences, and thus able to raise the level of their vibrations beyond that of the Pharaoh or any other person present. A mass hypnotism resulted in which these people were compelled to see things as they were imaged by these masters. Because of the attunement of Moses and Aaron, and the spontaneous creativity that seems to earmark much of God's action, they created an image which the magicians were not able to surpass.

On the second of August, 1939, a theatrical technician who listed his religious preference as "practicing the Golden Rule" was told he had been a magician in Pharaoh's court. An aptitude for "new ideas" stems from that life.

Before that we find the entity was in the Egyptian land when there were the persecutions, when the kings had forgotten Joseph.

There we find the entity was among those of the household of the pharaohs of that experience; and yet favoring the teachers because of the dreams, the visions, the interest in the magical things of that day. These brought to the entity much disturbance, and yet —as was experienced in the latter part of that sojourn —even with the departure of the children of Israel— the entity became more and more an adept in soothsaying; bringing to itself much of power and much of the ability to direct the lives and affairs of the many.

[*]*The Children of Mu* (New York: Paperback Library), pp. 212–13.

These then may in the present bring activities or abilities to direct many, especially in those things as would have to do with the creating of new ideas as for conveniences in the home, the office, or the store. These are activities through which the entity may gain the greater, the designing in woods or metals. These are the channels for expression for the entity.

But, first learn to govern self. Learn patience, learn mercy, learn judgment. Get understanding, and abuse it not. And when these are applied in the experience, we will find those abilities in those directions such— as indicated—as to bring harmony, peace, and understanding; and greater success materially, socially. (1974-1)

The following reading suggests the plagues of Egypt may have been a result of the life style of the Egyptians.

Consider the days of old, these are not foolish! When there were the families that produced upon the farm, how much better not only were the lives of the individuals but the character of the product—and there were not half so many pests to deal with!

And whence came they? From the same place that the flies and the fleas and the grasshoppers came to plague Egypt. (470-35)

A commentary on the ten plagues of Egypt was made by Edgar Cayce in his Tuesday Night Bible Class. This was not delivered in the trance state of his readings, but as a series of evening lectures.

"The judgments of God or Egypt were called plagues. We will consider each one in its proper order.

"First, the Nile is changed into blood. We might say the ten plagues are symbolical of the various stages of evolution. In our study of creation, it has been considered that physical evolution emanates first from

171

water. Man must spiritualize his creative impulses. In the last stage (the slaying of the first-born) it is only possible through the shedding of blood for redemption; in other words, sacrificing the individual life blood for the ideal. The pattern was shown to us through Jesus. Individually, we have our own shedding of blood to do. Not physically as He did, but in giving up our own purposes for His."

Symbolically, the "first-born" of any situation, from Cain on down, seems to represent the selfish impulses that brought about our involvements in materiality. What is the *first* reaction in a situation? Does it bespeak of self's spirit or the Christ's? The plagues remind one of Jesus' teaching, "There is no remission of sin save through the shedding of blood." It is only through tribulation and sacrifice that we shed selfishness from our activities.

"The second plague was the visitation of frogs. (Exodus 8:1–5) Frogs were particularly worshipped by many Egyptians, especially in the king's household. They were considered a great delicacy, and raised as food for the court. This visitation showed the Egyptians that the Israelites' God had the power to raise instantly that which took the Egyptians great care and time to produce.

"The third plague—the infestation of lice (Exodus 9:16)—demonstrates God's power to create living creatures, or insects, from an unnatural source. Lice are blood sucking insects, and would first have appeared upon the bodies of individuals or animals. Therefore, the Egyptians could not say the lice 'just happened' because of the unusual filth conditions. It could be said, however, that the lice were a natural result of the water having been turned to blood. The very moisture in the ground, if it were blood instead of water, would have made a natural breeding ground.

"In the fourth plague we find the first difference in the Egyptians' feelings toward the children of Israel.

The Egyptians were beginning to realize that the Hebrews were favored by a divine influence. (Exodus 8:30–32) Pharaoh was willing to permit the children of Israel to rest from their labors a few days and make sacrifices to their God. But Moses could not accept this. He knew he had to get the people out of the land entirely and away from the Egyptian influence.

"The fifth plague (Exodus 9:1–7) was striking at their source of supply. The disease on the cattle and the other beasts of burden was hitting at their pocketbooks.

"We notice after the third plague that the children of Israel were not afflicted as were the Egyptians. They seemed to be immune after that plague. Perhaps this indicates the Israelites had become so in tune with Moses' purpose that such things did not come near them. Today we still hear of people who believe that if they hold the proper mental attitude mice, flies, mosquitos, or any other kind of pest will not bother them.

"It has been indicated that the fifth plane of consciousness is the highest an earthbound consciousness can attain. This is interesting in the light of the sixth plague (Exodus 9:8–12) being the first the Egyptian magicians could not duplicate. It is also the first time these magicians could not immunize themselves from the plague's effects.

"Boils usually come from a condition of the blood. The blood had become susceptible to boils because of conditions resulting from the previous plagues. However, the children of Israel were immune. Possibly they were receiving guidance on how to keep their blood purified. We know that when we are sincere in our efforts, the next step is always shown us.

"The plague of the hailstrom (Exodus 9:13–35) was the first plague in which the choice of the individual became the governing factor. With the forewarning of the hail, every individual had the opportunity to choose if he would believe in the power of the God of Moses', or trust in Pharaoh's protection.

"This was the first time Pharaoh repented and admitted that he and his people were wicked. Human nature has not changed much from that day to this. As soon as things returned to normal, Pharaoh returned to his old ways.

"The plague of locusts is covered in Exodus 10:1–20. After the hail, the Egyptian people knew they should heed the warning about the locust. The people wanted Pharaoh to let Moses and his people go. They pleaded with Pharaoh. But Pharaoh could not concede. He had been taught from his birth that he was a god and all powerful. It was difficult for him to acknowledge his slaves' God was more powerful than he. It is also stated over and over agian, 'God hardened Pharaoh's heart.' Perhaps this indicates this particular ruler was working out his own destiny, according to what he had built in the past.

Pharaoh admitted his guilt again. Yet he went back on his word. It is hard to conceive of an individual who would not be completely overcome after being shown such things repeatedly in such a dramatic manner.

"Exodus 10:21–28 relates the ninth plague, Darkness. This plague signifies the spiritual darkness of an individual who continually refuses to recognize or use the light that is offered.

"Moses would not accept Pharaoh's conditions. When Pharoah, in his wrath, told Moses not to try and see him again, Moses said, 'Thou has spoken well.' Thereafter, Moses dealt directly with the people.

"Smiting of the first-born, the tenth plague (Exodus 12:29–30), produced greater suffering than all the others.

"Before the last plague, Moses was divinely led to prepare his people for their departure from Egypt. He knew the tenth plague would be the final one. The

Israelites were to cleanse their bodies by eating certain specially prepared foods. Their doors were to be marked with the blood of the sacrifice. God knew which were the believers, but this act gave the people a chance to express and show their allegiance.

After the death of all the first-born, the Egyptians were glad to lend the Israelites anything they had, just to be free of them. The Lord had told Moses beforehand that his people would not leave empty-handed.

Even when he told Moses to leave, Pharaoh asked for Moses' blessing. Evidently he now feared Moses and in awe of his power. Perhaps he wanted assurance Moses would not continue to call curses on him. Then, the Egyptian people, too, almost demanded that Pharaoh humble himself before Moses. This shows the power a people may exert, even under a monarchy. If sufficient pressure is created, the people CAN demand their rights. They were afraid that if Pharaoh did not accede to Moses' wishes, all would be dead. Also, the other plagues had not touched Pharaoh personally. The people had suffered because of their ruler's stubbornness. They were forced to work harder to keep him supplied with all things which he was accustomed to having. Consequently, the tenth plague, which took his first-born son, touched him for the first time."

A woman was told her interest in metaphysics and mysticism was a result of her Egyptian incarnation at the time of the plagues:

Before that the entity was in the Egyptian land, during those periods when there was the exodus of the children of promise from the land.

The entity was among the household of the pharaohs of that period. Hence all of the mysticism as wrought by that people, as well as the magicians of the own people, was a part of the entity's experience.

Thus, we find the entity INNATELY, as well as

175

manifestedly, is drawn to activities of the nature in which all such influences are a part of the experiences of individuals.

The name then was Zeta-Elda; and the entity gained. For though there were trials and sorrows, the activities innate brought the thought of—and the attempt to correlate—the relationships of man to man, with the relationships of man to the eternal influence. This brought great development, and abilities in the experience of the entity that may be applied in the present in an analysis of self and of that which forms the impetus for activities in the lives of others. (2185–1)

A poignant note is added in the following. Evidently, the last plague, the slaying of the first-born, touched her personally.

Q-8 Have I been associated in any past life with my son Junior, if so, when, where, and how?
A-8 As we find, the son was the brother in the Egyptian experience, and was among those taken when the death angel passed over.

Learn what THAT means also, as it may be analyzed, as to the experiences that have been a part of thy present relationship. How many sorrows, and yet joys and variations of same, in this relationship!

Joy may come out of same, if self holds to self-analysis and determinations. (2185–1)

Freedom!
"The Metaphysical Pattern"

The Edgar Cayce readings insist that, because man has been endowed with free will as a spiritual birthright, nothing but the nature of his desires binds him to any condition. If we listen to the mouthpiece of God within

(Exodus 6:9), instead of our own miseries and bondage, we can leave our "Egypt" anytime.

As an individual in any experience in any period uses that of which it (the soul or entity) is conscious in relation to the laws of Creative Force, so does that soul, that entity, develop toward—what? A companionship with the creative influence!

Hence karma, to those disobeying—by making for self that which would be as the tower of Babel, or as the city of Gomorrah, or as the fleshpots of Egypt, or as the caring for those influences in the experience that satisfy or gratify self without thought of the effect upon that which it has in its own relation to the first cause! Hence to many this becomes the stumbling block. (5753-1)

We need only sufficient desire, and enough faith to begin to trust to those ever expressive soul forces within, to be guided from experience to experience as we develop an ever-expanding mental-spiritual-physical consciousness.

Remember Cayce's statement that the Bible, from Abraham to Christ, is a pattern of mental unfoldment.

Hence, all that manifests in the material world is a shadow of that which is of mental or spiritual import. As to whether or not each division in mind, matter, becomes sufficient to be indwelling, or an at-onement with the Creative Force, is dependent upon the application of the purposes and desires of such force in its material association in materiality . . .

Then, the knowledge of the existence of such is the mental process. But the *application* of the source of each of these—as a premise in the experience—is that there is the willingness—of that which is the spirit, at an at-onement with the First Cause, or God, or

Creative Force—to be used . . . to produce that as the Creative Force would have signified or manifested in a material world—or constant desire, purpose, will, to be at an at-onement with the Creative Forces in its associations, in its dealings, in its relationships to its fellowmen. (1861–4)

This extract reiterates that the pattern of mental unfoldment is moulded through *service*, "the willingness to be used to produce that as the Creative Forces would have manifested in a material world," and through the seeking after truth, "the constant desire to be at an at-onement with Creative Forces."

These are the desires that will lead us out of the thrall of the appetites, the senses, or the ego.

But the first step toward freedom leads into the wilderness. Psychologically, once we decide to leave the narrow world of a habitual consciousness, we must confront the subconscious, the repressed and hidden areas of our mind.

"Mind is the factor that is in direct opposition to the Will," Cayce tells us. (3744–1) Like the complaining children of Israel, the old habit patterns, the conditioned thinking, our familiar and unquestioned attitudes and responses, will scream out with desire to return, to go back. Any step forward entails new responsibilities, new obligations. Often, we feel we would rather be bound in servitude, free from responsibilities.

This is our wilderness period. We cannot cross the Jordan into the Promised Land, where there are more battles to be fought, until the conflicting aspects of self are brought under the spiritual function of the Will. When we have the courage to take the responsibility for the *whole* body—spiritual, mental, and physical—raising it from servitude to service, we begin our Moses structure, another phase in that pattern "from Abraham to Christ."

The pharaoh within us, until weakened and humbled by the "shedding of blood," would keep the spiritual energy represented by the children of Israel, suppressed, using it for his own desires—to build his monuments and storehouses (Exodus 1:11). Once we can release this energy, and are willing to follow it, the intuitive soul forces within will lead us back to at-onement and The Promised Land, where we become ". . . with power temporal, power mental, power spiritual . . . Sons and Daughters of God . . . joint heirs with Him to the Crown of Glory." (262–36)

The crossing of the Red Sea is an emblem, or symbolic expression of the move into a new state of consciousness.

Q. Please explain the Master's statement to Nicodemus, "Ye must be born again."

A. When Nicodemus asked, "How can such things be?" the rebuke came in His answer, "Art thou a teacher in Israel and knoweth not these things?" Or, that *all* must pass under the rod, even as was given by those teachers that as Moses and the children passed through the sea they were baptized in the cloud and in the sea; as an example, as an omen, as a physical activity of a spiritual, a physical separation from that which had been builded in their experience as the sojourn in Egypt . . . Oh! that all would gather more of that understanding that the soul is a body and the physical is the mere temple, the mere shell, the mere material manifestation of that which may not be touched with hands! For it appears that we must be born again that we may dwell in those mansions not made with hands—but are prepared for those that have washed their robes, their bodies, their souls in the blood. For, ye are ones that may know the truth, if ye will but manifest in thine own experiences that ye have learned in thine meditations with thine God.

Ye must be born in flesh, in spirit again, that ye may make manifest that ye have experienced in thine own soul! (262-60)

The water of the river in Eden that divided in four heads was symbolic of a spiritual force entering in the earth. The water of the Red Sea indicates a cleansing, or baptism, as seen in this dream interpretation given by Edgar Cayce for a Jewish stockbroker:

Q. [Dream] Voice: "Now the water is come to wash it all away." I replied, "Aw, it has not. Why we aren't even finished our triangular battle."
A. In this is seen rather that of the spiritual forces as come from the superconscious forces to the subconscious in the representation of the deeper lesson as is to be gained from that as has been often given of old, "All shall be saved so as by water," see? for as the Children of Promise passed through the Red Sea and were all baptized unto Moses, in the Cloud and in the Sea, the lesson then is as of the cleansing of the physical forces to that pure water, that, as is given, to be the work of spiritual forces, or as is seen again as cleansing with the waters, see? for this becomes necessary in the putting away of those that so easily beset, coming nearer unto that perfect understanding of the spiritual laws of the God manifest in the physical world. (900-132)

Whenever we have obtained a separation (or salvation) from destructive forces, we should give thanksgiving. The experience should elevate us into a state of consciousness symbolized by a song of rejoicing, such as this one, the Song of Moses:

He is mighty and glorious, the Lord Jehovah has become our savior; he is our God, and we will praise

him; our Father's God, and we will exalt him . . .
(Exodus 15:2)

Miriam also rejoiced:

The Miriam the prophetess, the sister of Aaron, took a timbrel in her hand; and all the women went out after her with tambourines and with timbrels.

And Miriam answered them, "Sing to the Lord, for he has triumphed gloriously; the horse and his rider he has thrown into the sea." (Exodus 15:20–21)

The date of the following reading, July, 1924, shows it to be among the first Life Readings given by Edgar Cayce. A characteristic of these early readings is their briefness, no matter how notable or interesting the past experience may have been. This reading, for a young Jewish woman, suggests she may have been Miriam, the sister of Moses.

On the one before this, we find in the land of the Promise, where the children came again to the land of Promise from the bondage, and in this entity then we find the sister of the leader of the peoples who were brought from the land, and in this entity then [Moses] were the people led in the praise of Jehovah in the deliverance from the land. (Exodus 15:2, 20–21)

In this present we find the attraction to the hopes of the peoples' return to this promised land, and of the peoples again giving the message as of [the] promise to the world, as it will give. (2497–1)

The young woman was also told she had been among the Sons of God who were influences in the creation cycle of Genesis.

His final comment to her was:

Give then of self, putting this in the lives and in the hearts of all, only the spiritual forces and the soul development goes to Jehovah. (2497–1)

In the flight from Egypt, the 600,000 men, with their families, household goods, livestock, and all the things they "borrowed" from the Egyptians, must have extended over a large area. In the wilderness of Zin, they were able to group together as a congregation for the first time. Since their numbers were so vast, it was impossible for Moses to have direct personal contact with most of them. Perhaps most of them had never heard him speak. His pronouncements were probably relayed by other people, increasing the chances of misinterpretations and distortions of the original messages.

A young Jew, unemployed at the time of his reading, was told that in past experiences he had been a gambler in the American West, trained gladiators in Rome, and was a trumpeter in Jerusalem at the time of Ezra. He also had been one of those leaders in the Exodus who, through selfishness, rebelled, and brought destruction to the people.

Before that, we find the entity was in the land NOW known as or called the Egyptian, when there were those activities in the preparation of a people to be delivered under the leadership of the sons of Levi.

There we find the entity was among the relations and friends of the MOTHER of Moses and Aaron; and the entity—though among those who were in bondage— was raised to one as a leader in the Exodus.

The entity there gained something of the purposes of creative forces with the children of men, using same in corrective fields—as Zephaniah; and yet in the wilderness turning same to self again—which brought destructive forces into the experience.

But lean ye heavily upon the tenets of old, and the voice which ye heard in the pronouncements throughout those experiences there.

The entity, of course, was not among those who reached the promised land, but knew of the faults, the fancies, as well as the judgments of those through that period of thirty-odd years of journeying in the wilderness.

In the present experience, turn again to those counsels in the application of thyself and thy abilities in the present day relationships with others. (1881-1)

Shortly after the congregation assembled, the winds of rebellion began to blow.

> *And the whole congregation of the children of Israel began to murmur against Moses and Aaron in the wilderness;*
> *And the children of Israel said to them, Would that we had died by the hand of the Lord in the land of Egypt, when we sat by the pots of meat, and when we did eat bread to the full; for you have brought us forth into this wilderness to destroy the whole assembly with hunger. (Exodus 16:2-3)*

Two months after the experience in the Red Sea, the real enemy of the Hebrews emerged. (Exodus 16:3) Until now, it had been an external one, the Egyptian oppressors. But now the one that is *within* emerges. This enemy is much more deadly than their former oppressors, who fed and clothed them. The spirit of the Hebrews themselves could keep them embroiled in turmoils and forever wandering through a wilderness.

Manna

> *Then the Lord said to Moses, Behold, I will rain bread from heaven, for I will prove them, whether they will keep my laws or not. (Exodus 16:4)*

This entity, a niece of Aaron's, was both a helper and a rebel in the wilderness. A credence of legendary events stems from this life. Before that we find the entity was in the land now known as the Egyptian, during those periods when there was the cry of the people going up before the Throne of Grace because of the hardships as put upon them; for their burdens were heavy in those days.

The entity then was among these peoples, again of that one chosen as the priestly tribe, when the law by the leader—by the lawgiver—was given later in the holy mount. But the entity aided in carrying out those periods of purifications during those days when there was the making for the hardening of the heart of the leader and the setting in the minds of those children of the chosen ones as to the purposes for which they as a people were being called forth.

Then in the name Estrada, the entity was a niece of Aaron, the mouthpiece for the lawgiver. The entity gained and lost during the experience. For as there were the preparations, so did there come—during the periods in the journeys beyond the Red Sea—those periods of wonderment and rebellion in the experience of the entity.

Yet oft in the present the entity has felt that she has in some manner been a portion of many of those things that are recorded that others call but legendary tales. To the entity their truth may be made to mean, and does mean, much more than to many—if it will be let itself turn within. (872-1)

The memory and influence from legendary events remains with another entity who had been an Egyptian at the time of the Exodus:

Before that we find the entity was in the land now known as or called the Egyptian land, when there were those periods following the Exodus of a peculiar people.

There again we find the entity among those peoples who sought for the comprehending of the activities in other lands.

And we find the entity aiding in the preparation for

ways and means of the day for associations and connections by physical activity and associations.

Hence the preparations and manners of travel—and yet ships and waters are a part of the experience, as have been the experiences of the entity in its dreaming or day dreaming—the visions of the things or conditions that would influence men and nations in their activity toward those things as were handed down in manners such as even legendary folklore or legendary powers as attributed to individuals for their own development, but the greater for the release of influence or power for their fellow man.

The name then was Hep-Su-Tun. (1782–1)

Manna

Then the Lord said to Moses, Behold I will rain bread from heaven, for I will prove them, whether they will keep my laws or not. (Exodus 16:4)

In *Worlds in Collision*, Dr. Immanuel Velikovsky advances a scientific reason for the physical manifestation of manna. In the following, Cayce gives us an interpretation of mental and spiritual manna. If they so chose, the children of Israel could partake daily on all three levels.

Remember, as He said to His disciples, "I have food, I have strength ye know not of." In giving of His strength to the woman at the well, it brought that heavenly food that satisfied the soul, that makes the growth, that brings the at-onement, yea, the atonement to the soul. And this ye may have, if ye will apply thyself in the better, yea in the broader sense. For those are thy stepping-stones. Do not let them become stumbling stones. (540–18)

... as each entity under a given name makes its correlating of that it does about the Creative Forces in its experience, it is coming under those influences that are being fed by the manna—*which is a representation of the universality as well as the stability of purposes in the Creative Forces as manifested to a group or a nation of peoples.* (Author's italics.)

So it becomes that as the Master gave, "Ye shall not live by bread alone, but by every word that proceedeth from the mouth of the Father."

That indeed is the holy manna which each entity, each soul in each experience must make a part of its mental and spiritual self. (281-31)

One of the hardest lessons to be learned is the lesson of thanksgiving. Being thankful for whatever occurs to us keeps a way open, through our trust and humility, for the mental, spiritual, and physical "manna" which will be supplied each day sufficient for the need.

It is well that ye be reminded, then, of how—in those periods when there were the preparations in the lives and experiences of a peculiar people, under unusual circumstances, in extraordinary environments— they were reminded, not in their days of plenty but in the days when each day they were given only sufficient for that day, that periods were to be, should be, set aside when thanksgiving was to be a part of their activity—their remembrances for all the joys, the sorrows, the disappointments, the hopes that were and might be theirs if—IF—they would but hold to those promises; relying—as it was necessary in those days, those hours, for a complete dependence—upon the bounty of a merciful Father, who had a purpose in the bringing out, in the edifying, in the directing.

And today, as ye look back upon those experiences, ye—TOO—find thyselves chosen.

Have ye chosen Him?

For as was given then, "If ye will be my people, I will be thy God."

This is a universal experience, then. To each soul

gathered here, to each soul throughout the land, to each soul as may be in all lands: "IF YE WILL BE MY PEOPLE, I WILL BE THY GOD!" (3976-21)

Joshua's Love

Early in the trek, we glimpse a deep personal experience of Joshua, the soul who later became the Christ. It was events like these, the early death of his betrothed, that helped shape the destiny of his soul as he underwent all the experiences of man in the earth.

On June 16, 1944, a nineteen-year-old Jewish girl was told:

... the entity was in the Egyptian land when there were the activities in the preparations for the exit from Egypt to the favored land, the people through whom was chosen the hope of the world.

The entity was then the close friend of Joshua. Yes, one of those to whom Joshua was engaged, as would be called in the present, and of the daughters of Levi, not the same as Moses and Aaron but rather of Korah. There we find the entity beautiful, lovely, beloved of Joshua and yet weak in body, because of conditions under which the entity had in a portion of its experience labored, and thus weak-lunged, passing away during the period of the journey to the Holy Land.

But to have been beloved of Joshua was sufficient to have builded, into the personality, that individuality of the entity, that which still makes the entity beloved of all who know the entity best, loved by all its companions, it associates, just as in those experiences with the great leader who was to carry the children of promise to the Holy Land.

The name then was Abigal. (5241-1)

Two years before the above reading, the parents of an eleven-year-old boy obtained a reading for their son.

They were told the boy [2779] had been the brother to this girl and a friend of Joshua's.

A hint of the suffering and tragedy of his sister's death, in that life, is expressed in the following, as Cayce describes the boy:

One that is at some periods as a tyrant in self, and yet so tender, so gentle, so understanding as not to be able to see the least thing suffer. And a real proof of this, as may not be experienced in any other association would be for the entity to come in contact with an individual suffering in the last stages of what is called T.B. or consumption; for through such there might be seen even a flare-back to the period of the greater manifestation and awakening of this entity in the material plane. (2779-1)

That life of great manifestation and awakening was described as follows:

Before that the entity was in that land when there were those preparations for the journeying of the children of promise from the Egyptian land; when the leaders Moses, Aaron, and Hur brought about those experiences.

The entity then was of the same age and an associate of Joshua, who became the spiritual leader even to Moses in the interpreting of his experiences in the activities through that journey; as well as the companion of Joshua.

For, the entity then was the friend of Joshua, being the brother of the girl whom Joshua loved, yet who on the journey—before the wedding—died of tuberculosis. Thus that innate feeling, the entity will find, may be expressed in hearing of, reading of, ANY persecutions; and especially of the suffering of those from tuberculosis.

The name then was Jarael. The entity experienced

turmoils through that sojourn. Yet, when there were those experiences after the hardships and the early portion of the journey, when there were those meetings between Moses in Mount Sinai, Joshua's interpretation to Jarael brought the greater spiritual concept—and aroused much of the entity's experience in the material sojourn before that.

Then the entity gained and became as a leader, as one who—with many of its associates or companions in the present—may, with some direction (dependent upon the suggestion made), become AGAIN as a leader and a director in this material experience. (2779-1)

Some Jewish scholars claim that the real complainers among the children of Israel were not the Hebrews, but Egyptian "hangers on" who followed Moses. They were the ones who were in disfavor in their own land, and used the opportunity to escape their fate by joining with Moses. Most of the children of Israel, the Jewish commentators feel, had faith and did not question Moses' guidance. They were familiar with the concept of God as Spirit. The Egyptians, who were used to having material forms as images to worship, needed constant reassurance that help could always come from unexpected and unforeseen sources. They needed the miraculous to make them realize the Israelite God was to be experienced rather than seen.

The Life Readings indicate Egyptians did accompany Moses, and many Egyptians, even those in authority, were favorable to the Hebrews.

Before that the entity was in the Egyptian land when there were those of the children of promise leaving the cities of Egypt.

The entity was an Egyptian—not of the people of promise, or of the Jews—as they were even called then, or Hebrews—but the entity was favorable to those. For, the closer friend of the entity was the associate of Joshua—who was so ill when they left, or when they were preparing for the leaving, and who died on the way.

Then the entity was in the name Shalmahr, and the entity was among those close to those in authority and power in the land. For the entity's companion and its associates were in rule over those people, though the entity was favorable—as indicated—to the Jewish or Hebrew women, especially. (1635-3)

These remarks were made by Edgar Cayce in his Tuesday Night Bible Class:

Moses and Joseph married the daughters of Egyptian high priests. No mention is made of Joshua's marriage. Although the physical lines of Joseph and Moses were not the channels through which promise of Christ's coming was fulfilled, their spiritual influence and teachings far surpassed those who did keep to the pure physical strain. Evidently Joseph and Moses came into the earth to perform the tasks they did. It was not important to them or to the future welfare of their people that they conform to the letter of the law. Yet for others, it seems very important that they obey the law physically. A thing is right for one person and not right for another—depending upon the ideal or purpose for coming into materiality. There are times when individuals are not required to keep to the letter of the law. It is always necessary—and possible—to seek to show OURSELVES approved unto God and His purposes.

Joshua did marry, as this brief comment from a physical reading indicates.

In the mental and spiritual body, keep in self the ideals that were set by self in much of its [the soul's] association through the various periods in the earth; as was seen especially as the wife of Joshua—as a close association with the Master: "Let others do as they will or may, as for me and my house, we will serve a Living God." (573-1)

A request for a Life Reading was made, but circumstances intervened, and it was never obtained.

Jethro's Contribution

Moses encamped at Sinai, at the mountain where he had the burning bush experience. When Jethro, his father-in-law, knew where Moses had settled, he came to see him with Zipporah (Moses' wife) and his two sons.

Jethro was a descendant of Abraham and Keturah, and was familiar with the form of worship and sacrifice taught by Abraham.

Edgar Cayce, reading for an elderly Protestant businessman, saw in his soul's experience several lives where he had significant roles in great spiritual, moral, and political movements. He had been in the colonies at the time of the American Revolution, and had participated in all the discussions with the great leaders about separation from England. In a Roman incarnation before that, he had, as a powerful Caesar, helped spread the empire. And before that, he had been Jethro, Moses' father-in-law.

. . . we find the entity was among the princes of Midian, or a Prince of Midian—Jethro, the father-in-law to Moses; and to him was given the abilities to counsel with the elders of the peoples who gave not only the ordinances as to material conduct of the elders but much as pertained to the manners of preparation of sacrifice.

For the entity then was not only as a counselor to that people who became as leaders to the world because of their religious forces and influences but to those who came to many another land. (1266–1)

When Jethro appeared, he saw Moses bogged down from morning to evening, judging all the controversies and complaints of the people. Jethro was able to make wise use of his abilities to "counsel with the elders." He aided Moses in establishing the appointment of seventy men who were to be chiefs over thousands. They were to carry out all the detailed matters, and leave Moses free for more important things.

With all his ability and guidance, Moses needed the practical suggestions made by his father-in-law. The Lord uses everyone who is willing to be used. No man could do what Moses had to do unassisted. As a priest, no doubt Jethro was divinely guided.

The following readings belong to several of those elders who were selected at that time.

Hur was one of those chosen. Hur is an important figure who is twice mentioned in Scripture. He stood with Moses and Aaron on the mountain top, upholding Moses' arms, while Joshua led the Hebrews in their first battle against the Amalekites. (Exodus 17:10)

Later, when Moses and Joshua went on the mountain to commune with God, Aaron and Hur were left in charge of the congregation. (Exodus 24:14) Hur's grandson was the craftsman Bezaleel, who supervised the construction of the Tabernacle (Exodus 31:2)

In 1943, Edgar Cayce told a Danish executive he had been that gifted leader:

Before that, the entity was in the Egyptian and Palestine land, when the first counselors were selected for Moses, Aaron, and Joshua and those that led the people to the Promised Land.

Then in the name Hur, the entity carried forward those activities in a manner bespeaking the keeping of a well organized effort on the part of the many groups, and even the personalities to be dealt with, even as indicated in Moses and Aaron and Miriam as well as Joshua and the sons of Korah and the rest of those leaders at that period.

Study those tenets also especially in Exodus 19:5. There is the basis, my friend, of those things in which ye may excel. (3435-1)

A young woman requested a Life Reading and was told she once had been Hur's daughter, and evidently made positive contributions.

. . . the entity was in the Egyptian land, when there were those preparations being made for the journeying from the land.

There the entity was in the household of Levi, and a recorder—as would be termed today, or a helper—to Moses and Aaron; but the companion—or the daughter—of Hur.

In the experience the entity became acquainted with much that had to do with the ways, means, and manners of controlling groups, and those who find fault with the interpreters of the law as well as those who interpreted the attempts of the Creative Force to bring the consciousness into the lives of individuals of His purpose with man.

There the entity became something of a politician, as would be termed today, as well as an instructor in the ways of those who would keep their own household intact.

Then the entity was in the name Shebeth, and the entity gained much that may be applied in the present in that of teaching, or in analyzing individuals or individual problems. Apply these abilities in the spirit of creative energies, not as for self nor for the gratifying of some appetite of body or of mind-mental. (2796–1)

Her present husband had been associated with her twice before, in experiences with Israel.

Q-4 When, where, and how have I been formerly associated with my husband?
A-4 In Egypt, as in association with Hur; as in the promised land in the activities there. Not very good friends in the one—very close in the days of David. (2796–1)

Of the "able men" which Moses chose (Exodus 18:25–26), there was one who did not always make wise judgments. Cayce saw in the soul of the person a deep urge for atonement and penance, in part stemming from this experience.

Before that we find the entity was in the earth during those days and periods when this chosen people from the Egyptian land journeyed toward a land of promise, and when Moses chose the seventy elders that were to be judges among thy brethren.

The entity then was of the household of Reuben, chosen as among those that acted in these capacities; in the name Eleasiah.

In this capacity, judgments were not always the best. And when those days came when Beth-Korah made for rebellions, we find the entity was among those not called but who gave his counsel, being moved by the promptings that had been in the experience through the very associations of those experiences in the mount.

Thus we find those changes coming over the entity then, and the later days were spent in what has often been felt within self; whether it is to be an atonement, at-onement, or penance.

Choose rather the *living* way, that ye may know Him. For God hath not mocked man, but the premises have ever been, "When ye call, I will hear" if ye are in earnest; if ye are in doubt—*fear* has crept in! (1238-1)

The Encampment at Sinai

When the Lord told Moses he would speak to him on the mount, He gave Moses and the people three days to prepare themselves for the visitation. (Exodus 19: 9-11)

Perhaps three days has no symbolical or special significance, but it did give everybody an opportunity to prepare themselves. Many did not make the preparations and consequently were not allowed to participate.

And it came to pass on the third day in the morning that there were thunders and lightnings and a thick smoke appeared upon the mountain and the sound of the trumpet exceedingly loud; so that all the people that were in the camp trembled. (Exodus 19: 16)

The thunder and lightning left a deep impression on this soul.

. . . before that the entity was in the Palestine land as a companion to Miriam, who aided in directing spiritual precepts, yea in the tenets of the law that Miriam's mother and brethren gave to those peoples.

The days at Sinai brought misery, brought strength, brought power. And the entity is still afraid of thunder and lightning, yet such has its attraction. The Lord is in the storm, for He is the Lord of the storm also.

The name then was Shushan. The entity was among

the daughters of Aaron, and thus one of the household and understanding of the priesthood. (3659-1)

And the whole mountain of Sinai was smoking because the Lord descended upon it in fire; and the smoke thereof ascended like the smoke of a furnace, and the whole mountain quaked greatly.

And when the blast of the trumpet sounded long and grew louder and louder . . . the Lord came down upon Mount Sinai, to the very top of the mountain . . . and Moses went up. (Exodus 19:18–20)

This reading creates a vivid picture of a literal, historical happening:

Draw a comparison, my son, as to what has been given you. Does this not stand much in that same position as illustrated in those days when the people waited? Though they had seen the Lord Jehovah descend into the mount, they had seen the mount so electrified by the presence of the God of the people and ohm of the Omnipotent to such an extent that no living thing could remain in the mount or on same, save those two who had been cleansed by their pouring out of themselves to God, in the cleansing of their bodies, in the cleansing of their minds. And yet they tarried only a few days, their cry to the leader was, "We know not what has become of this man. Show us another way. Why cannot we return rather to the gods of the Egyptians. Make thou one that shall lead us, for we know not what has become of this man." [Exodus 32:1]

Thou hast been shown a way, a perfect way, whereunto thou mayest cleanse thyself, thine body. Why seekest thou to find another god that may lead thee, that is made whether of gold, stone, wood, or what not? Why not be patient my son, and prepare thine self that thou mayest in the very spirit of truth manifest the perfect way. Not a fault in thee, no. Thine overanxiety, or—as was expressed by another teacher—the very zealousness of thine self may eat thee up and destroy the real value of that thou mayest be in thine zealousness trying to do! Oft has it been given, "Stand ye still and see the glory of God." Let *Him* have his way with thee, that thou mayest indeed know thou art guided step by step with His ways.

Then, as to the healing or the aid, if thou workest together, let *Him* guide; not *thou* seeking through another channel, or even *this* channel, to do other than He has prepared—or the ways He would prepare thee for the best thou mayest do. (440-16)

Edgar Cayce brought out the following points in his cussions with the Bible class:

"The burning mountain was also the place where Moses saw the burning bush. The mountain was charged with electricity. The people then knew a constructive side of electricity that we have lost today. Those who did not know the laws of it could easily be destroyed, just as one could today.

"The vibrations were raised so high, that those who were not attuned could not stand it. The area was 'roped off' to prevent sudden death to those who might accidently overstep the boundary. Moses led the people in a period of meditation, or a devotional, to better prepare them for what they were about to witness. All the people could hear the thunder and see the lightning. Perhaps some even sensed the meaning of it. But only a few could hear the voice.

"Even with the three days of preparation, the priests were not able to go into the mountain with Moses and Aaron. Either they were not sufficiently attuned, or completely sanctified. To be in an attitude of prayer, or going through certain forms of purification externally is not enough. Our LIVES must be in accord with what we are seeking. We must be attuned to those vibrations which are necessary for receiving spiritually. This is what Jesus meant when he told us to ask in His name—not to ask just with words, but by living our lives as He lived his. If we do that, we can ask and it will be done."

The Ten Commandments

The following commentary is taken, once again, from the records kept of Edgar Cayce's weekly Bible class:

"It is well to picture in our minds how the ten commandments were given and who was with Moses at the time. The rest of the Bible is written around this chapter. Even the Sermon on the Mount, given by Christ, is just an extension of it.

" 'Thou shalt have no other gods before Me.' No individual is to be considered before God. This is probably the most violated command of them all. We do not consider ourselves idol worshippers, but it is hard not to think first of ourselves and our own wishes above all else.

"This is our great trouble today, as individuals and as a nation. We want what we want. WE WANT to be all power. WE WANT to hold on to all the MATERIAL POSSESSIONS we have, regardless of everything else. Can we say, 'Thy Will Be Done,' and mean it, when our desires and material possessions are at stake? Jesus said if we try and save our life, we shall lose it. It behooves us to heed this commandment, to try and practice it in our daily life.

"Notice the first few commandments pertain to our relationship to God. The rest are about our relations with our fellow man.

"The second commandment: a graven image could be anything to which we have so much importance as to be all encompassing for us. It might be position, fame, money, prestige, or any material desire that outweighs our desire to be a channel for God's manifestation and glorification.

"Non-Catholics feel it is sinful to make a statue of the Virgin. Orthodox Jews feel Christians are disobeying the second commandment when they worship Jesus as the Christ. Yet they look on the patriarchs and prophets of old as messengers of God and examples to follow. There is a difference between an object you worship and an example you live by. Jesus promised a day would come when we would worship God in spirit and truth. Until we reach that state of consciousness, we will need constant reminders before us to help us reach the goal we are striving for.

"What is meant by 'a jealous God'? It is necessary at times to use certain words to convey certain meanings. Jealousy was and is a thing that is understandable. Perhaps this is only another way of saying, 'What ye sow so shall ye reap.' It indicates certain laws are set in motion according to our actions, which bring about definite results.

"Visiting iniquities of the fathers upon the children of the third and fourth generations was refuted by some of the later prophets. Ezekiel disavowed the proverb that the sour grapes eaten by the fathers would set the children's teeth on edge. He stated each soul was accountable for his own sins. The theory of reincarnation might explain how a soul might come back into the third or fourth generation of its own strain to materially reap what it had sown.

"The third commandment: Jesus said we should not swear by the temple, for that is where God lives. If we say harsh things against others, perhaps it is the same as taking God's name in vain. We all are divine in Him.

"The fourth commandment: an individual must decide for himself how he can best keep the sabbath. The sabbath was intended as a day of rest, in which appreciation could be shown for the blessings of the week. Our manner of doing this depends upon our purpose and what we consider showing appreciation. Rest does not mean just sitting and holding our hands. More often it means a change in the way you think. Whatever we feel is right, we should live up to it.

"There are seven centers in the endocrine system of the body. These centers are centers through which spiritual impulses enter into the physical body. They act separately and collectively. They must coordinate if we are to remain balanced. It has been indicated by some, that it is absolutely necessary to give a seventh of our time to serious contemplation of our spiritual natures, else we cannot keep a balance.

"The fifth commandment: 'Honor thy mother and father; that thy days be long upon the land which the Lord Thy God has given thee.' To honor your parents is to think of them before yourself, showing them preference. This is the first commandment with a promise. If you truly honored your parents and respected them, you probably would desire to live longer, and your life would be in keeping with the purpose you had in entering this life.

"'Thou shalt not kill,' the sixth commandment. Jesus told us that we can kill with anger. In fact, to kill 'one's spirit' with anger, a harsh word, pessimism, or any other form of negativity is a violation of this commandment. We are meant to be constructive and creative, not destructive. We should not destroy what we cannot give.

"'Thou shalt not commit adultery.' According to Jesus' interpretation, the seventh commandment refers not only to the physical act of adultery, but to any thought which would contaminate or separate us from the purity and spiritual unity for which we are striving.

"The eighth, ninth, and tenth commandments are self-explanatory. We must remember that there are extremes in the material sense of the law, but not according to the spirit of the law as given by Jesus. In Him the extremes meet."

A newspaper woman was told she was one of the first who heard and applied those new commandments.

For the entity was among those that journeyed from Egypt to the Holy Land, when there were those chosen to act in the capacity of the judges in the various tribes.

The entity in the name Abarther, of the tribe of Asher, was among the first to comply with those judgments at Sinai, when the records and the laws were given to those peoples in the particular land. The entity kept those judgments through the period, being among those that were also helpful to Joshua before the entering into the Promised Land.

The entity was not among those who entered in, but those who paved the way for helpful forces during those preparations for same. This gives the entity in the present experience very peculiar ideas concerning political favors, but it will be hard for the entity to be a machine person. Yet it will be necessary in the experience, if the entity would comply with the rules, especially in those areas from which it may seek such honors. Change rather the ideals of thy constituents, and you'll mean much as their representative. (3486–1)

The Tabernacle

Along with the ten commandments and the laws and ordinances which Moses received at this time, he also was given the perfect pattern for the tabernacle of worship for the living God. According to Cayce, every facet of this tabernacle has a spiritual, mental, and physical relationship to the body of man. The body is the temple, the readings stressed.

Another newspaper woman, a Christian Scientist, learned in the wilderness the meaning of the temple.

Before that, the entity was in Egypt when those peoples entered into the Holy Land, now called the Jewish or Hebrews.

Then the entity was among those selected to be in charge of those activities that dealt with the preparation of the temple in the wilderness, or the tabernacle that eventually became the temple.

And, as the entity has learned in the present, the body is indeed the temple, and that the pattern given in the mount is that pattern of the individual entity or self as it is set up and hedged about, and yet is the place where man meets his Maker.

The entity then became one well grounded in those tenets and truths, the weaknesses of the material needs oft overshadowing the entity, yet in those periods of the close walk with the leader who entered into the land there was brought peace and harmony into the experience.

Then the name was Elded. (3129-1)

Many people were required to execute the minute directions and details outlined in Exodus 25-27. Cooperation between the tribes was necessary, because all tribes were involved.

A six-year-old Ohio boy was told he had been a craftsman from the tribe of Dan:

Before that, we find the entity was in the land now known as the Holy Land when the peoples journeyed from Egypt to the Holy Land.

The entity was among those who aided some of the sons or children of Dan to prepare the mechanical things for the carrying of the tables, the altar, candlesticks, and those things which were to be used by other individuals.

The entity was then in the name Eijalu. In the experience the entity gained the more, and with the application of self came knowledge and power within self to control influences about the entity. (5153-1)

Psychologically, the work demanded they recognize a state of perfection.

That discipline still remains with this particular entity, who was also of the Danites.

Before that, we find the entity was in the periods when there was the journeying from the Egyptian land to the Promised Land and when there was the choosing of the individuals who were to prepare the various elements which were to be used in the hangings in the preparations of the tabernacle in the wilderness. The entity was then of the tribe of Dan and in the name Segualar prepared the cloth which was the first veil between the Holy of Holies and the Ark itself. [Exodus 26:31–33]

Thus the desires latent in self to be superlative in its work, to be honored in the office to which it may be assigned or to which it may be aspiring. But know there are those applications of such in which they must be made tenable judgments between individuals. (5392-1)

The directions for the completed tabernacle are both symbolic and literal. The intricate anatomy of our physical bodies represents a reflection of a spiritual pattern, which we can find within ourselves.

The symbolic relationship between the body and the temple is drawn here:

The entity finds self a body, a mind, a soul. These are as the shadows which were indicated in the mount by the outer court (the body), the inner court (the mind), and the still more holy of holies (the soul). (2067-1)

Q-9 Is the temple here the physical body?
A-9 Rather the *mental* in which is the pattern as of the tabernacle; or the holy mount—or that as set by a *unified* service of the body-mind, the body-physical, the body-spiritual; that vehicle that is without nails (as was the tabernacle as a pattern), not bound together, yet a covering, a place, an understanding for a *unified* activity with Creative Forces, or the power of God. The veil without, the holy within, and the holy of holies—knowing that there must be the cleansing, there must be the purifying, there must be the consecration. All of these are as patterns, they are as conditions, they are as experiences for each and every soul.
Q-10 Is the court referred to the body apart from the spiritual centers?
A-10 As indicated, rather is it as the environ without —the body—physical and mental within for its sacrificial forces, and then to the spiritual force within as to the holy of holies. (281-32)

The inner relationship to the outer pattern is further discussed in this psychic reading:

In the expressions as shown in the tabernacle, in the orders as given for its construction—the size, the shape, the measurements, the figures above the holy of holies, the directions of the colors as indicated for the hangings, the manner in which each board was to be set, the manner in which each skin was to be used or dyed—these were not only for the physical protection but for the expressions that would come in the experience of individuals that took the service of worship there as being a thing within themselves. Hence became material, emblematical, and the experience of the application of same in the worship there became as a living thing in the experience of the individuals. (338-4)

In the book of The Revelation, much of the symbolism is based on Old Testament experience. The Revelation was closely investigated by friends of Edgar Cayce, and many psychic readings were given in order to interpret it correctly. Through the series of readings known as the 281 series, they discovered how much of the Old Testament patterns and symbols relate to forces within the perfect structure of man.

Symbology of Two

And you shall put the mercy seat on top of the ark; and in the ark you shall put the testimony that I shall give you.

. . . and I will commune with you from above the mercy seat, from between the two cherubim which are upon the ark of the testimony . . . (Exodus 25: 21–22)

The two cherubim have a strategic position in the place of communication. Perhaps these two angels have the same metaphysical significance as the two witnesses in Revelation 11:3. The two witnesses were interpreted by Cayce (281–33) as representing motivations which arise from outside the physical being—the astrological, or mental, influences—and the emotional forces which are produced from incarnations in the earth.

These then are the witnesses. The innate and the *emotional; or the spiritual-mental, the physical-mental;* the subconscious, the superconsciousness. (281–33)

Could these two cherubim "above the mercy seat" represent the same two forces?

Symbology of Ten

Moreover you shall make the tabernacle with ten curtains of fine twined linen, and blue and purple and scarlet material; with cherubim, the workmanship of a craftsman shall you make them. (Exodus 26:1)

The symbology of ten is suggested in the following:

Q–10 What was meant in a previous reading by this statement: "For he that sings, he that sees, he that speaks, he that hears well is especially gifted of God; and not only has the one or the two but the five talents that may be made into such measures, by the choice of the entity, that he may be ruler not only over the five senses but the ten kingdoms in God's own way"? A–10 It was meant what was said. Just as that indicated in the parable of the talents by the Master. He that used the five talents was given more. He that uses the five senses—as of speech, of song, of hearing, to the GLORY OF GOD is given the ten to use or to rule over—as was the man with the talents. (622–7)

If these curtains represent the ten senses of man, then the veils are an appropriate symbol. This shows they are still "behind the veil" and hidden from all but the Seeker.

The Mercy Seat

And you shall make a mercy seat of pure gold, two and a half cubits long, and a cubit and a half breadth.

And you shall make two cherubim of gold, of cast work shall you make them on the two sides of the mercy seat. (Exodus 25:17–18)

. . . that ye ARE—that of good—rises ever as an incense, sweet before the throne of mercy . . . that which has been kind, gentle, patient, merciful, long suffering in self's experience during a day, rises before the throne of the mercy seat within self to that of an incense of satisfaction. (281–30)

The mercy seat was a symbol to help the people understand what they were to expect of God. They didn't understand it then, and too often we don't today, Cayce told his class. God is Love, and in His Love is kindness, patience, and understanding. We will never know the meaning of mercy until we understand God's mercy to us. The best means of obtaining this awareness is to practice showing mercy to others.

Mr. Cayce's thoughts on these aspects of temple symbology were delivered to his Tuesday Night Bible Class as follows:

"To have our bodies and minds conform to the same pattern as the temple outlined in Exodus, it is necessary to do certain things uniformly and with the proper attention to detail. But not so ritualistic as to forget the spirit or purpose behind the rite. The daily ritual should remind us of the necessity to make our lives in accord with our spiritual purposes.

Some part of our day should be dedicated to meditation, to entering into the holy of holies within ourselves. We should prepare ourselves for this communion with the highest forces known. We need to make a habit of doing those things each day which will keep us in remembrance of the fact that the body is the temple. THERE He has promised to speak with us."

These thoughts are given by the unconscious Cayce on entering into the holy of holies within self:

For as [was] given of old, how oft must that associate of the entity [have] been lonely; that man of God who waited long upon the mount, [who] gave to those peoples of old those commandments as from Jehovah Himself? Lonely? Yes, in the physical sense; but that as he gave stands ever as the judgment of man to his Maker, "There is set today before thee good and evil, life and death. Choose thou." Thus has it come to all who waited then with him, and as his successor gave, "Let others do as they may, but as for me and mine, we will serve a *living* God."

With that attitude, with that purpose, with that intent in the dealings with thy fellowmen, there will come a peace, a harmony, and an understanding that —as has been given—is not known by those who seek not to do His ways. (1238-3)

For, "My spirit beareth witness with thy spirit" is an immutable, an unchanging law. And again, the heavens, the earth may pass away, but His laws shall not pass away.

Hence, in thy seeking, find that answer; not as from something without, but from opening the door of thy own consciousness to the promises that are sure in Him. For ye will find that as the pattern which was shown in the mount to Moses, as well as the greater pattern in the temptations to Jesus upon the mount; in that indeed as He was lifted up, He draws all men (and this means women also) unto Him. (2067-1)

Do stay close to the Ark of the Convention, which is within thee! (5177-1)

Keep that as indicated. Let the strength of self not be wavered by advice of the many; but turn to the within, knowing that the POWER lieth there!

For when ye enter into the holy of holies, in thine own self, there ye may find STRENGTH that is beyond compare of man's physical abilities. (1752-1)

And you shall erect the tabernacle according to the right pattern thereof which I have shown you on the mountain. (Exodus 26:30)

Aaron's Breastplate

And Aaron shall bear the names of the sons of Israel in the breastplate of judgment upon his heart when he enters the holy place, for a continual memorial before the Lord. (Exodus 28:29)

Each precious stone in Aaron's breastplate carried the vibration of the tribe it represented. The messages from God pertaining to each tribe were interpreted by Aaron according to his understanding of the emanations from the stones.

Well that the entity have the stones or minerals about self when in periods of meditation; or in those periods when it may find itself more easily attuned to the influences that may use the body, either in the healing forces that flow through—through its attunements, or through the visions and the associations of the entity . . . (688-2)

A warning was given regarding stones:

These do not give the messages. They only attune self so that the Christ Consciousness may give the message. Listen to no message of a stone, of a number, even of a star; for they are but servants of the Lord and Master of all—even as thou. (707-2)

In Babylonian mythology, certain gods were messengers to mankind, and wore upon their breasts "Tablets of Destiny." Through these stones the people could inquire of their gods for yes and no answers to questions concerning their destiny as a nation and the fate of their kings. This is an interesting parallel with the Israelites. Aaron, as high priest, and the spokesman for Jehovah, and the breastplate was used exclusively in matters concerning the king or nation. Perhaps, in earlier days, the use of stones as a means to attune to a higher consciousness was very widespread.

Each element, each stone, each variation of stone, has its own atomic movement, held together by the

209

units of energy that in the universe are concentrated in that particular activity. Hence, they come under varied activities according to their color, vibration, or emanation. (531-3)

Urim and Thummin

And you shall put in the breastplate of judgment the Urim and the Thummin; and they shall be upon Aaron's heart when he enters before the Lord. (Exodus 28:30)

Urim and Thummin have been interpreted in a variety of ways, from "purity and perfection" (Lamsa) to "revelation and truth" (Jewish Encyclopedia).

Certainly the high priest had to strive for "purity and perfection" in his heart in order to receive "revelation and truth." This is applicable for us in the present.

The true importance of Urim and Thummin is that they were aides, a helpful means through which the priest could attune his consciousness to the Divine.

Q. Is there any likelihood at the present time of developing a machine based on the action of the electro-magnetic cell, which may assist in securing direct communication as done by Aaron and Moses—and many others—with Urim and Thummin?
A. Find in self that as Hatherpsut put to self, in knowing who should be chosen—yet the trouble arose.* Do not make the same mistake, that the vibration is the force—but that which impels same from the Creative Force. Such machines are claimed to be made. Some do, some do not, create the right vibration. Too oft does there enter in those personalities of those seeking.

Then, in self, find the way to aid; and call again on Ra-Ta, and on Hatherpsut—they are as Urim and Thummin, a channel only. (355-1)

*See p. 158-59.

Hence intuitive force is the better, for in this there may come more the union of the spirit of truth with Creative Energy; thus the answer may be shown thee, whether in Urim, in Thummin, in dream, in numbers, in *whatever* manner or form. For He *is* the strength of them all, and beareth witness *in* thee and through thee—if ye but do His biddings. (261-15)

A Michigan housewife [987] had once helped prepare the legendary breastplate. When Cayce viewed her record in the psychic state, he saw her love of God symbolized by a golden cord which ran through all her experiences from the beginning of time. The cord represented the central desire of the soul, and served as a link which connected all her experiences into each other. Her present life could be her last earth experience, Cayce told her, unless she chose to enter again on a mission, or a service, for God.

Her activities in the Wilderness helped build that consciousness, and are described as follows:

Before that we find the entity was in that land, that period, when the chosen people were being given upon the holy mount the manner of their exercise in the temple, or in the service before the tabernacle.

The entity then was among the daughters of Levi, and those chosen to make the vestment of the priest. And to the entity, because of its own abilities, there was given the preparation of the setting of the breastplate and the putting of the stones thereon, and the preparation of the Urim and Thummin for the interpretations of the movements that came upon the high priests in the holy of holies to be given to his people in or from the door of the tabernacle.

Then in the name Henriettah, the entity's activities were in a high force *equal to* the cousin Miriam.

Throughout the experience, the entity gained; for it reasoned with Nadab and Abihu; it counseled for

211

Korah, yet did not allow self to become entangled in any of those influences that would have made for the rise to the position of fame. Rather did the entity choose to remain as one in the background that there might be given the greater understanding to that mighty people as they stood in the presence of the I AM that had brought them to the holy mount.

In the present from that sojourn, those things pertaining to the mysteries of the temple, the mysteries of numbers, of figures and those things that have their hidden meaning, become as a portion of the entity. Yet oft does there arise that sudden change as to the fearfulness of people giving too great a power to such things that would lead them astray; as they did in the experience of the entity in the wilderness. (987–2)

Strange Fire

Know then that the force in nature that is called electrical or electricity is that same force ye worship as Creative, or God, in action. (1299–1)

Free will is as powerful as electricity, and can be a force for evil or good, depending on our use of it. Through their knowledge of the God-head and its energies, and the vibrations they raised in worship and devotion, the Hebrews could electrify a mountain, part the sea, or make water spring from a stone. Misuse of this tremendous force resulted in death, as it did for Nadab and Abihu.

This reading makes use of the symbol of "strange fire" which Nadab and Abihu offered on the altar of the Lord. (Leviticus 10:1)

Many having lost sight of the purposes, the ideals, have presented strange fires upon the altars of truth. These are necessarily blinding to those who would remain, even in the straight and narrow way. Be not blinded to those conditions that easily beset each individual, yet there must ever remain that loving care, that perfect differentiation between those [who] would build for constructive influences in the lives of those who would associate themselves in carrying forward that of truth, that is life itself, as is set in Him who has ever presented a way for a more perfect relationship between the Creator and the creature. (254-52)

And there went out fire from before the Lord and devoured them and they died before the Lord. (Leviticus 10:2)

Remember the pattern in the mount, in self, in the physical body, in the mental body, in the spiritual body. *That* is the mount! So long as there is perfect coordination in the mount, all things work together for the *good* of the mount. When there is the rebellion in the mount, then there is disconnection, destruction, disconcerted effort, and the coordination—the cooperation of activity—is made awry. Hence death in the physical ensues, by the disintegration, through disconcerted action, through the *incoordinated* action —and this mental, and physical, and spiritual.

So, in overcoming all He set that as the Throne, or the mercy seat that is within the temple, as the pattern, as in the mount . . . "I will arise and go to my Father, in Him, through him. *I will! I will!* (282-36)

The subject of this reading was a young Jew who listed his beliefs as "non-orthodox":

Before that the entity was in the earth during those days when the peoples were returning from the Egyptian land to the Promised Land.

The entity was among those of the household of the sons of Levi, and close to the sons of Aaron; being then a companion to one of those destroyed because of offering strange fire—Abihu—then in the name Ashua.

With those periods of turmoil that arose within itself, the entity found dissension; yet becoming later the companion of Ithamar's son, the entity brought the bettered conditions when there came the periods of preserving and maintaining for those of the priesthood a unity of activity in their temple service, directing in the separating of each group for definite services.

In the present from that experience we will find that those engaged materially in such activities as a service in temple, or in teaching, or in directing of the spiritual life, will be particularly attracted to this entity; though the entity will hold such afar off. It would be well to consider same during the twenty-sixth and twenty-seventh years in this sojourn, for in those periods the entity should think of marriage. (1204-3)

In this reading, we find the *wife* of Nadab:

Before that we find the entity lived in the earth during those periods when there were the preparations for the journey to the Promised Land.

Again the entity was in one of the families of the Levites, nigh unto the household of the leaders in that experience; being in the household of those who were then friends, neighbors, and associates of Jochebed, the mother of Moses.

These associations with the mother brought the entity into close association and activity with Miriam and Aaron, during those periods that the entity Moses joined closer with the activities and relationships with his own people.

During the period of [the] sojourn through the wilderness, the entity then became nigh unto the priesthood again; becoming then the wife of Nadab, one of the sons of Aaron made the high priest.

With the destruction of these in the Wilderness of

Zin because of their offerings of strange fire on the altar, it brought to the entity the widowhood which made the longings for the changes that were gradually wrought by the activities with the sons and the daughters of Jethro, those that joined themselves later to the activities.

And the sons then of the tribe of Judah became the protectorate to the entity during the rest of its experience in that sojourn . . .

In the present these make for conflicting influences at times in the experiences of the entity. Yet join into the services in the tabernacle, for these mean much to the entity. (325–63)

Mrs. 325, the wife of Nadab, in her present incarnation was the mother of Mr. 257, for whom the following reading was given.

Before this the entity was in the land where the peoples were become the separate and distinct people, and was of the priesthood of that people, and in that time was he one of those offering strange fire upon the altar.

As to these conditions as brought in the present sphere, we find first.

Those that bring the entity's soul and spirit forces close to the worship of the Jehovah, yet holding itself ever afar from giving of its best, or of its first self, to these natures.

In the second that of the strength of the elements necessary for the insight, yet with the first giving that peculiar bend to the insight as not understood by self or others. Hence, the mighty force of will to know self, and understand self, if it would make the best in the present plane. (257–5)

There is an interesting parallel between the present Mr. 257 and his life as Nadab. Mr. 257 was a personal and long time friend of Edgar Cayce, and was one of the key men upon whom the responsibility fell for establishing the A.R.E. Through this friendship, he could fulfill the vital role he had neglected as Aaron's son.

The following reading was obtained by Mr. 257 for guidance in respect to his role in furthering the work of Edgar Cayce.

The karmic implications of his present condition are drawn by Cayce. At the reading's conclusion, Mr. 257 is put on notice that his responsibilities are an opportunity —and a necessity—to cleanse himself of the egoism that led him astray as Nadab.

Q-3 Should [257] plan to devote his entire time to the work as he planned and how can he accomplish it now?

A-3 Rather not as he has planned. Let him prepare himself as God has planned. Be a channel of blessing, not tell the forces nor God how to do His work . . . Rather be that channel through which individuals may be given an opportunity to approach the throne itself, and cast not thine pearls before swine nor so conduct thine own self that thine good is evil-spoken of nor thine evils are good-spoken of . . .

As conditions of the material natures clarify themselves, as they will, do not mix material conditions with spiritual forces. Do not attempt to serve God and mammon. Do not serve thine neighbor with one hand and draw from his pocket with the other. Rather let thy yeas be yea and thy nay be nay, knowing that [what] is given for the increase is from the Giver of all things.

Q-4 From whom came this beautiful message?

A-4 From self. Oft has this very condition confronted self, as to whether to be able to put on again those royal robes, and to prevent from offering the strange fires on the altars of the throne, has come to the self;

and would the entity, the soul, be again associated in that love that makes for purity before the throne, the decisions in the flesh must be made.

Q-5 What can [257] further do in his daily life to show himself more approved unto the Giver of these gifts?

A-5 Study to show thyself approved unto God, avoiding the appearances of evil, knowing that as the acts of thine going-ins and coming-outs are that reflection of the God ye would serve; if that God be money, power, position, fame, these must reflect in . . . the life [and] the acts of self. Will those forces be manifested as were made manifest as of old, when Abraham [was] called to go out to make a peculiar people, a different nation, so again may the body hear that call as when offering in the temple, that "Mine people have wandered astray," yet in the little here, [in] the world there, the precept and example, they may again know Jehovah is in His holy place.

Q-6 Who was [257] during that period of Abraham?

A-6 Walked with Abraham.

Q-7 Is the name given?

A-7 One who stood at the tent when the call was that as given, "I will make of thee a strange nation." Not in the flesh. Later in the flesh as was seen when the body [257] offered strange fires on the altar in the word of mouth in that [which] led many astray. *Now the body [is] given the opportunity in this experience to make for a cleansing of that experience.* (5502-3) [Author's Italics]

In rabbinical literature, two opposing views are taken concerning Nadab and Abihu. One views the brothers are prometheans who purified themselves and made the supreme sacrifice to bring Divine Fire into the congregation. Less romantic (and more nearly correct, according to the readings for Mr. 257) is the other which holds the brothers were consumed by their own self-esteem. They considered themselves superior to Moses and Aaron and were jealous of their leadership. They also felt they were too good to be married.

This entity learned a great lesson from Nadab and Abihu's intemperance.

Before that the entity was in the Egyptian land, being among those journeying from Egypt to the Holy Land. There the entity was among those associated with the high priests, for the entity was then the wife of Abiathar. The relationships to Aaron and to Nadab brought unusual experiences, when there were the activities first setting up the service in the tabernacle. From these lessons the entity, then Abijah, found the necessity of being convinced within self, and of keeping in what may be termed the straight and narrow way.

These periods brought to the entity the extreme disturbance through a portion of the sojourn, and again those activities that set the entity as one in authority throughout that period of journeying through the wilderness; aiding in the choosing of those helpers to Abiathar, as well as the other sons of Eleazer who led in those activities after the happenings in the wilderness. (3416–1)

Who Were the Enemies?

And it came to pass, when the ark set forward, Moses said "Arise, O Lord, and let them that hate thee be scattered; and let thy enemies flee before thee." (Numbers 10:35)

Ye have no enemies. Let this ever be within thine own heart: Do *right* in self, and that which is thine own can not, will not be taken from thee. Those who try such are enemies to themselves. Look not upon them as enemies to thee. Feel sorry for them for their misconstruction of right. (3250–1)

Moses prayed that *God's* enemies be scattered, not his own. The Bible gives no indication who the enemies were. Was it an external enemy—something perceived from afar? Or was it his own people who bore a spirit at enmity with God's?

Shortly after this prayer, several more rebellions occur. In one, the issue was meat. (Numbers 11) In another, a personal issue was provoked by Miriam and Aaron, his own brother and sister, over Moses' marriage to an Ethiopian.

An Opportunity to Enter

After a three day journey, Moses was told to select individuals, in whose judgment all Israel had confidence, to spy out the Promised Land.

After forty days they returned, bringing fruit from the land and a good report. They said the land flowed with milk and honey. The cities were fortified, and ". . . we saw giants, the descendants of giants; and we were in their sight like grasshoppers." (Numbers 13:33)

The giants were the remnants of those beings who had entered into materiality outside the line of Adam.

In the matter of form, as we find, first there were those projections from that about the animal kingdom, for the *thought* bodies gradually took form. These took on *many* sizes as to stature, from that as may be called the midget to the giants—for there were giants in the earth in those days, men as tall as (what would be termed today) ten to twelve feet in stature, and in proportion—well proportioned throughout. (364-11)

If this is true, then we can understand why it was necessary for this line to be destroyed, and why Joshua (who had been Adam) had the responsibility to do so. Once they were slain, and their race extinguished, they would have to reincarnate through those channels which were the result of the creation of Adam. Their souls

219

then could begin on the upward process of evolution.

God had promised the children of Israel these tribes would be destroyed. He promised them possession of the Holy Land. Now they were being tested as to whether they were willing to stand on those promises.

Before that the entity was in the land when there were those activities during the journeying from Egypt to the Promised Land. Though the entity was not among those who reached the Promised Land, he was among those who were the defenders of those causes to which the two [Joshua and Caleb] were engaged who reported the ability of the group—or Israel—to enter in at once.

The entity was also of the tribe of Aaron, or of Levi; but not of those that were ever active in the temple—more as those that cared for the temple activity.

Thus the entity was acquainted with those conditions which had to do with the preparation by Moses, by Joshua, by Aaron, and by those in authority, as to the manner in which the groups were to be formed in their march.

Thus certain routine, certain activities always become a part of the entity's experience; the desire that right things be in their right place, and that right things should follow in a consecutive way or manner. These become as latent and manifested experiences for the entity.

The name then was Shem—of the brethren of Moses and Aaron; of that group dedicated for a special service in activities in that direction.

Keep the faith, then, as well indicated there. For those who seek are indeed Israel, and Israel indeed is ALL who seek; meaning not those as of the children of Abraham alone, but of every nation, every tribe, every tongue—Israel of the Lord! That is the full meaning of Israel.

In the present, then, we find that there may be that systematic use of those tenets as superscribed there by the lawgiver himself—these may be well applied in the present. (2772-1)

But the men who went up with him said, We are not able to go up against the people; for they are stronger than we.

And they brought up to the children of Israel an evil report of the land which they had spied out, saying the land through which we have gone to spy out is a land that devours its inhabitants; and all the people that we saw in it are men of a giant stature. *(Numbers 13:31–32)*

Cayce opened his reading for a young dramatic arts teacher [3463] in a most unusual manner, saying, that the entity was someone who "will either make something so unusual as to almost startle the world, or he won't amount to 'a hill of beans'!" In order to make this contribution, Cayce said the young teacher must gain confidence in himself, by having confidence and trust in the purposes of the divine. Thus he could make amends for many shortcomings in past lives.

Before that the entity was among those journeying to the Promised Land, among those peoples chosen to spy out the land, and was with the leaders who returned with the good report.

The entity was persuaded by the greater number that there was not the ability to conquer or to overcome. The name then was Japin. The entity lived through that experience regretting the rejection of those convinced within self by the Holy Spirit [of] God, just to be on the popular side for the moment. The entity again and again regretted the declaration that the optimism of Caleb and Joshua was foolhardy.

Thus in the present there may be the warning, Do not reject that thou knowest in thine heart, mind, and soul to satisfy a moment of gratification, of being popular, or being upon the popular side. But know that self is right, and that it is in keeping with the divine within self. For there is within each soul, each entity, that image of the Creator—if there is the attuning of the self, the ego, the I AM to the divine—which may enable nothing to hinder the entity from accomplishing, attaining any position of power that is the desire of the heart. But use it aright. Forget not the declaration made by him whom ye rejected that led those people into the Holy Land, "Let others do as they may, but as for me, I will serve the living God." (3463-1)

In Atlantis, [3463] was among the children of the Law of One, but joined with the Sons of Belial and "brought death, destruction, sin, and ugliness in many, many ways." He turned away from a ministry of education through love, kindness, and patience to gratify selfish desires, and rejected all warnings given by the spokesmen from the holy sources. By supporting Caleb and Joshua in their favorable report of the Promised Land, and uniting with those who were convinced by the Holy Spirit, he had an opportunity to correct those weaknesses which had begun in Atlantis.

His lack of confidence has been a result of a failure to stand firm and has remained a pattern in succeeding lives, although he did gain spiritually as a martyr in Roman times.

He was warned by Edgar Cayce, if he turned from the way of truth and light to gratify self's desires and vanities, "Woe be unto the entity, not only here [in this life], but in those experiences to come."

This particular reading supports the hypothesis that many of those who were with Moses in the wilderness were the Sons of God who had come with Adam in the beginning, but had fallen away from their spiritual purposes. The Wilderness period gave them the opportunity to re-establish their relationship to God, which they either accepted or rejected.

> Then all the congregation was in commotion; and lifted up their voices and cried; and the people wept that night.
> And all the children of Israel murmured against Moses and against Aaron; and the whole congregation said to them, Would God we had died in the land of Egypt! Or would God that we had died in the wilderness!
> Why has the Lord brought us into this land, to fall by the sword that our wives and children should be prey? We were better off when we dwelt in Egypt. (Numbers 14:1-3)

For two years the children of Israel had been listening to Moses and Aaron preach. They had gathered the commandments of God under which they were to live. They heard all the prophecies. As slaves, they were used to having others make decisions. Now they were forced to make one themselves. Had they sufficient courage and faith to face the adversaries God had promised them they could subdue, they could have entered and taken possession of the Promised Land. Fear ruled. They rejected God's promises. Thus a long period of wandering began.

Korah's Rebellion

Throughout the years of wandering, Moses was plagued by one rebellion after another. The people grumbled when their stomachs were empty, and complained when thirsty. Even Aaron and Miriam rebelled when Moses married an Ethiopian woman. Still other rebellions occurred when factions, such as Korah's, began to question Moses' authority and his right to be their leader.

> *Now Korah, the son of Izhar, the son of Kohath, the son of Levi, and Dathan and Abiram, the sons of Eliab, and On, the son of Peleth, sons of Reuben, started a faction.*
>
> *And they rose up before Moses with certain of the children of Israel, two hundred and fifty chiefs of the assembly, who at that time were men of renown;*
>
> *And they gathered themselves together against Moses and against Aaron and said to them "Is it not enough for you, seeing all the congregation are holy, every one of them, and the Lord is among them; wherefore do you lift up yourselves above the whole congregation of the Lord?" (Numbers 16:1-3)*

A missionary woman, whose husband had become an alcoholic, was told:

> Before that the entity was among the chosen people journeying to the Holy Land. The entity was among, close to, the sons of Korah, that one who rebelled; not Korah, but the son of Korah—Zipohar.
>
> The entity in the present is again meeting self in the condemning of others, for, again the pattern is the withdrawal from companionship because of unbelief, unfaithfulness.
>
> In that experience the entity suffered in mind, gained in principle and in the patience that will yet be tried as by fire. (3179-1)

There is more than one instance when individuals questioned Moses' authority. Even after the miracles they had seen him perform, they disputed whether God had really chosen him or not.

And Moses spoke to Korah and to all his company and said to them, In the morning the Lord will show who are his, and who are holy; and he will cause them to come near to him; and those whom he has chosen will he cause to come near to him.

This do: Take for yourselves censers, you Korah, and all your company;

And put fire into them before the Lord tomorrow; and it shall be that the man whom the Lord chooses, he shall be holy; this is enough for you, O you sons of Levi. (Numbers 16:5–7)

We must constantly make tests within ourselves as to which is God's way. As long as we are not fully convinced by the Spirit, there is always the possibility of being deceived by others, or the subtleties of our own egos. But if we truly are sincere, we can bring it all before God—and by this test and the results, know which is the true path, pattern, spirit, or leader to follow.

The test should be as within self. For read thoroughly, analyze the admonitions given by the lawgiver after his experience of the period of activity in the earth—one and twenty years had the entity been given to giving the law, the moral law, the penal code, the marital law, relationships of all kinds. Know indeed the knowledge is latent within. (5377–1)

Edgar Cayce speculated with the class.

"It seems to us that if we had walked across the sea on dry land we never could forget it. But when we look at ourselves and think we have come a long way, we realize that perhaps we are not much farther advanced in many ways than these people. Often we vow to ourselves that we won't do so and so, then we forget it before the sun goes down."

This entity sided with its family through duty, and was able to gain spiritually.

"Before that, the entity was in the lands when there were the journeyings from the house or land of bondage to the free land, or to the land of promise.

"The entity then also was of the lineage of the Levites, but of the Korah tribe, being among the daughters of the sons of Korah.

"In that expereince the entity gained, and yet held to its duty to its father and mother, which brought destructive experiences in the activities of the entity in its youth, though the entity was not destroyed when those of the household of Korah were destroyed. However, resentments were builded in a manner that found expressions again, without due consideration to the spiritual experiences of the entity.

"Thus the necessity in the present—for the TRUTH of spiritual life and spiritual processes as related to the material AND mental forces—for the entity returning to a physical, mental, and spiritual understanding in order for there to be a normal balance.

"The name then was Ashbahel."

This entity learned a lesson from Korah, and also gained spiritually.

"Before that, we find the entity was among those peoples who journeyed from the Egyptian land to the Promised Land.

"The entity was among those who were of the sons and associates of Korah, but not of the Levites who were destroyed. Being young in years during the experience, the entity learned a lesson, and became among those who joined with the Gershonites as the keepers of moneys, or the records of same, until there was the division of the lands in the Promised Land.

"Hence, we find the entity in the present is one that

may be a very good statistician, or datastician, especially as to things pertaining to the working of or working with things made of wood—as varnish or finish, of form, or shape, or molds, of things that would have to do with ornaments for same.

"For as one of the Gershonites, though of course, as indicated—of the kinsmen of Korah—the entity gained throughout that experience; and was close to the elders as they established their activities in the Promised Land.

"Hence, there is the great desire for knowledge pertaining to those who are in high places—the innate urge to be TRUE to all influences, and yet—as it were—seeing the shady tradings of those about the entity, the upper hand as taken because of weaknesses of some character or nature in the associates or friends or the activities with others; but be not tempted by same.

"The name then was Ajlon."

And Moses said, Hereby you shall know that the Lord has sent me to do all these works; for I have not done them of my own mind.

If these men die the common death of all men or if they be visited after the visitation of all men, then the Lord has not sent me.

But if the Lord make a new thing, and the earth opens its mouth and swallows them up with all the things that belong to them, and they go down alive with all that belongs to them into Sheol, then you shall know that these men have provoked the Lord.

And when Moses had finished speaking these words, the ground split asunder under them;

And the earth opened its mouth and swallowed them up with their households and all the men who were with Korah and all their goods. (Numbers 16: 28–32)

227

This woman was among the faction who were "swallowed up."

Before that we find the entity was in that land now called the Egyptian, during those periods when there was the Exodus of the people from that land going into the Promised Land.

The entity then was among the daughters of Aaron, that was the teacher with Moses the leader, the son of Egypt that with his peoples chose to carry those things forward. The entity kept well into the teachings in those experiences. And when there were the rebellions when the sons of Korah were destroyed, the entity had turned rather to those things that bespoke of the adding to, even as the brethren had done, when Nabad and Abihu offered strange fire. The *entity* offered strange fire in those things that became an abomination in the days of Korah, and the earth swallowed up the household of Abazeal, the daughter of Aaron. For in that experience did the troublesome things that make for the aggrandizement through position and power, the aggrandizement of selfish interests, bring those things of defiance to the lessons and tenets and applications of extremes in a material world.

In the present, we find from the experience innately, the periods of rebellions that arise. Hence, the necessity of those injunctions that have been shown: learn ye patience! Bear ye one with another and thus wholly fulfill the laws of love, for these are they whose feet shall walk in the pathway of light and lead many aright. Go not after the strange paths that lead into destructive forces even as Korah. (683-1)

They, and all that belonged to them went down alive into Sheol, and the earth closed upon them, and they perished from among the congregation.

And all Israel that were round about them fled

228

at the cry of them, saying "Lest the earth swallow us up also."

And there came out a fire from before the Lord and consumed the two hundred and fifty men that offered incense. (Numbers 16:33–35)

This reading raises the question, just how did they die?

Before that, the entity was active in that period when there were the journeyings from Egypt to the Promised Land. And the entity was among those who defied the leader, who set in question as to whether those authorities were only given to one individual or not, and not answered, though as the record is given, destroyed; but not in the way and manner as would be indicated by that character of record presented, but as in the fact of the self being allied with those that did defy—NOT God, but the authority of a man.

In that experience the entity followed close with the true tenets of truth, that the law is a universal consciousness and is applicable in the experience of each soul that seeks the truth in his relationship to the Creative Forces, or God—an influence within and without, that must answer by the manner in which ye apply same in your relationships to others.

Thus the questions as to the sincerity of individuals or groups—this oft becomes the measuring stick of the entity in the present. (3031-1)

This entity, a Jewish male, sided with Joshua and Moses in the dispute.

Before that, we find the entity was among those peoples born in the wilderness during the journeying of the children of promise to the Promised Land—during those days when there were disputations as to those activities of Korah.

We find the entity standing close with those of Joshua, Aaron, and Moses to the defense of the activities through those experiences of the purifying of body for the dedicating of same for a service in the activities of the peoples as they journeyed.

There we find the entity gained, throughout that experience; being one that upheld those tenets, those principles, those ordinances as were proclaimed during those experiences.

And from that experience, those abilities to bring quietness out of dissension, the abilities to quell those activities that would become mob activity, those abilities to counsel with those who are individually sad hearted, come as a natural activity of the entity.

The name then was Shulzar. (1856-1)

Desire is fire, and it purifies. As long as we create a desire to be at-one with God, no matter how many rebellions or complaints we make—no matter how many diversions we insist upon in our wanderings—eventually we will achieve the object of our desire. A state of peace and unity with God and man. It is a law. As long as there is the constant desire, and striving, there will be the achievement, and "forty years" shall come to an end.

The Stumbling Block at Meribah

And there was no water for the people to drink; and they gathered themselves together against Moses and against Aaron.

And the people quarreled with Moses and with Aaron, saying, "Would God that we had died with the death with which our brethren died before the Lord."
(Numbers 20:2-3)

Edgar Cayce's comments to his Bible class were simple and pragmatic on this lesson:

"When they needed water, they blamed Moses instead of turning to God for guidance and direction. Each time Pharaoh refused to let the people go, Moses didn't doubt what God had already told him. He went back and asked God what he should do next. If his people had followed Moses' example, things would have been much different."

And Moses and Aaron gathered the congregation together before the rock, and he said to them, "Hear now you rebels; out of this rock we will bring forth water for you."

And Moses lifted up his hand and struck the rock with his rod twice; and the water came out abundantly. (Numbers 20:10–11)

More lessons were drawn for his students:

"Because of all their complaining and backsliding, Moses must have felt very superior to the rest of the people. He said 'Must *I* give this rebellious people water to drink?' One of the hardest lessons to learn and manifest is humbleness of spirit, especially when one is in the position of authority. With all his abilities, Moses had not conquered himself. He took unto himself the glory of giving the water."

For these are at those periods when . . . there *must* be the *disseminating* or the giving away of the egoism of self. Consider as an example in thy study of same, the servant Moses. For these become as may be found even for and from that record as ye have, the stumbling block at Meribah. (281–29)

The following commentary suggests Moses' transgressions at Meribah may have been the breaking of the first commandment.

Q–8 Can [257] receive donations from people he has introduced during the past years?

A–8 Provided [257] presents same as a *service* to mankind, and not as "I accomplish so much for so much." Let the body-mind, the body-consciousness, gain this lesson: that "I must be made one with the *I AM*," rather than the I made to appear as the representative of the *I AM*, see? For let that mind be in *you* which was in Him as he gave those lessons as were written upon the tables of stone—for this begins with the first and the greatest commandment of all: set not *self* in seeking or in obtaining, or in any manner set self beyond or a *judge* of *any* man's, or of any *individuals*, or of any ideas above and beyond that first set, "Thou shalt love the Lord thine God with all thine heart, thine mind, and *thine body!*" (257–20)

Another Detour

And Moses sent messengers from Rakim to the King of Edom, saying "Thus says your brother Israel, you know all the trouble that has befallen us;

How our fathers went down into Egypt and we have dwelt in Egypt a long time; and the Egyptians oppressed us and our fathers;

And when we prayed before the Lord, He heard our voice and sent an angel, and has brought us forth out of Egypt; and behold, we are in Rakim a town in the uttermost of your border;

Now let us pass through your land" . . .

But Edom said to him, "You shall not pass through my border, lest I come out against you with the sword."

. . . and Edom came out against them with a strong force, and with a strong hand.

Thus Edom refused to give passage through his

border, wherefore Israel turned away from him.
(Numbers 20:14–18, 20–21)

Isaiah proclaims we must make straight a path in the wilderness. This could be interpreted from a metaphysical point of view to mean the establishment of a pattern of activity that leads us directly to God. We must travel through the depths of our own subconscious minds to build that highway that will establish a permanent connection with the superconscious forces.

As we seek to make a straight highway through the subconscious to these higher forces, often we may uncover pockets of suppressed, rebellious energies which create long detours.

This inner pattern is represented externally in Numbers 20, when the Edomites would not let Moses pass through their lands. Thus they could not go "straight" in their journey, but were forced to take a detour of endless, barren miles.

Two of those Edomites are represented in the following:

Before that the entity was in the land where the activities were carried on, when the children of Promise passed through the land that they were forbidden to pass through, save with permission.

For the entity was among the descendants of Esau. Thus one that looked to the products of the field, and the abilities to use the mountainside in the interests of those things pertaining to mining, herding, though then as a leader.

The name was Jared. The entity took advantage of a group. Hence, expect a group to take advantage of thee! For what ye measure, it must be, it will be measured to thee. For ye must pay every whit that ye measure to others. And this applies in the future as well as in the past. Do ye wonder that your life is in such a mess!

233

From same in the present, then, ye will find things pertaining to spirituality, a search for truth, coming nigh unto thee, even as then. Do not disregard same in the present. Lay hold on same. Seek Him while He may be found. (3063–1)

In the one before this we find in that land when the peoples were returning to the Promised Land. The entity then among those who hindered their return through Edom, and of the Edomites. Then in the name Gibdden, and the entity gained and lost in this period—gaining in that of the manner of the entity's service, losing in being of the oppressive disposition, or using will force in that direction against self's own judgment.

In the urge from same is seen that the entity uses those conditions of religious force and position in an erroneous manner, for rather than preparing self to meet the needs of same, attempts to bend same to meet the needs of present day conditions. (2676–1)

An Intimation

And the Lord sent fiery serpents against the people, and they bit the people, so that many people of Israel died.

Therefore, the people came to Moses and said to him, We have sinned, for we have murmured against the Lord and against you; pray before the Lord, that he take the serpents away from us. And Moses prayed for the people.

And the Lord said to Moses, Make a fiery serpent of brass, and set it upon a pole; and it shall come to pass that everyone who is bitten by a serpent, when he looks upon it, shall live.

So Moses made a serpent of brass, and set it upon a pole, and it came to pass that if a serpent had bitten any man when he beheld the serpent of brass, he lived. (Numbers 21:6–9)

Edgar Cayce saw in Numbers 21 an intimation of Christ's death on the cross.

This reading gives the basis for Cayce's insight.

Get a hold upon self. Read, study, to know by heart, that given, "In my Father's House are many mansions. Were it not so I would have told you, for I go to prepare a place, that where I am ye may be also, and I—if I be lifted up—will draw *all men* unto me. Even as Moses lifted the serpent in the wilderness, and he that looked was healed from within—he that looketh on me, as I am lifted in that consciousness of the individual that the soul hangs upon that clarifying of the life from *all* forces of the material forces, may be lifted up and enlivened from within." (4757-1)

The readings insist we have the power to heal ourselves, if we will only believe the power lies within.

Eventually the brazen serpent became a stumbling-block, just as any symbol that is abused and misunderstood.

Balaam

In Numbers 22, the children of Israel are very close to the Promised Land. They are encamped on the east side of the Jordan, opposite Jericho. Balak, the king of the Moabites, was afraid they intended an invasion of his domain. As a protection, Balak sought out Balaam, a famous psychic of the time, in order to have a curse pronounced upon the Israelites.

Balak believed if Balaam pronounced a curse, the very worst misfortune would fall upon Israel. Balaam was a prophet, who was possibly schooled in the lore of Egypt, Persia, and cults further eastward. He also was acquainted with the worship of God as proclaimed by the Israelites from the time of Abraham.

Balaam must have valued his psychic abilities, for he

wasn't intimidated by Balak. He told Balak he could only say what God allowed him to say. He wouldn't attempt to sway the message to suit Balak's desire. This indicates Balaam recognized the power he had came from a higher source over which he had no control. No doubt he hoped the information he received would be favorable to Balak because it would bring great material gains. But he knew not to force the issue—else it would be to his own undoing, and the riches would mean nothing.

At night, Balaam received a message from God—perhaps in a dream or through the trance state.

> And God came to Balaam at night and said to him, "If these men have come to call you, rise up and go with them; but only the word which I shall say to you, that shall you do."
> So Balaam rose up in the morning and saddled his ass and went with the princes of Balak.
> And God's anger was kindled against him because he went; and the angel of the Lord stood in the way for an adversary against him. (Numbers 22:20–22)

This is one psychic's commentary on another: Edgar Cayce's Bible lesson follows.

> "Did God go back on his word? If He told him to go, why did He send the angel to block the way? Was He angry? Perhaps Balaam was so anxious to go, because of the possibilities for material gain, that he misinterpreted God's message. Often we persuade ourselves we are doing the right thing when we are not, because we are so intent on having our own way."

> And when the she-ass saw the angel of the Lord, she lay down under Balaam; and Balaam's anger was kindled, and he stuck the she-ass with a staff.
> And the Lord opened the mouth of the she-ass and she said to Balaam, "What have I done to you that

236

you have struck me these three times?" (Numbers 22: 27–28)

Cayce comments to his Bible class:

"Unless we count the serpent in the Garden, this is the only reference in all Scripture to an animal speaking. Many animals are very close to the universal consciousness and can sense and see things man does not. When the ass spoke, Balaam answered it in a most natural way. Perhaps he didn't realize this was a genuine psychic experience. When he realized what was happening, he fell on his face, possibly fainting and losing consciousness."

In a reading for an astrologist, Cayce found:

. . . the entity was in that land wherein the children of promise entered on their journey to the Promised Land—in Midian. The entity was among the daughters of the prophet that was called to curse Israel and was spoke to by the beast as well as warned in those experiences.

These brought the entity to a better interpretation and to the study of the laws recorded through the activities of those peoples.

In the latter portion of its sojourn the entity sought activities that brought better relationships, before there was the full destruction of those peoples that hindered. The entity joined then with those that made terms later in the Promised Land.

The name then was Elzjah. (3356-1)

Evidently this astrologer was also involved in spiritualism as the following question infers.

Q-3 Was Odenatus of Palmyra, who is now Meah "over there," my true mate?

A–3 The true mate was the one that was in the Midian experience, when there had been the acceptance of those activities in the Promised Land. It was not Odenatus but Demetrius that was the brother of Odenatus. (3356–1)

Balaam Succumbs

Although he failed in his effort to have Balaam pronounce a curse on Israel, Balak evidently was able to bribe Balaam to devise an ingenious plan which resulted in the death of thousands of Israelites.

In his commentary on Balaam, Edgar Cayce suggested Balaam's eagerness for material gain may have been the reason the Lord rebuked him after giving Balaam permission to go with the men of Moab. Cayce's view probably originated from two sources—his own insight into human nature, and two New Testament references, 2 Peter 2:15 and Jude 1:11.

Revelation 2:14 refers to Balaam as the one "who taught Balak to cast a stumbling block before the children of Israel to eat things sacrificed to idols and to commit adultery."

This suggests Balaam had a part in enticing the Israelites to participate in the sensual pagan rituals of the Midianites.

And Israel abode in Shittim, and the people began to commit whoredom with the daughters of Moab.
And they invited the people to the sacrifices offered to their gods, and the people did eat, and worshipped their gods.
And Israel joined herself to Baal-peor; and the anger of the Lord was kindled against the children of Israel. (Numbers 25:1–3)

The spell of these self-indulgent attractions drew many thousands of Israelite men into the Moabite camp where the laws and moral code established by Moses were wantonly disregarded.

The whole of Israel seemed threatened by this mass defection. In a moment of righteous indignation, Phineas, the grandson of Aaron, stayed the plague in a most dramatic manner. Zimri, a respected leader and prince of Simeon, had entered the tent of a Moabite woman, Cozbi. Phineas followed him, and thrust his spear through both of them while they were engaged in the sexual act. The people were stunned by the example made of these two. The fear of God rose in them, and they returned to their priests, listened to their counsel, and refrained from the temptations offered by Moab.

According to our present standards, Phineas took upon himself a great responsibility, killing two people in the name of God. Yet this decisive act was exactly what was needed to restore order and to prevent the complete dissolution of Israel.

Does it seem fair that two should bear the punishment for the sin of thousands? Apparently the soul of Zimri gained from that experience by being used as an example:

Before that the entity was among the children of promise, as they journeyed from the Egyptian land to the Promised Land.

The entity was a prince among his own people, but one whose activity was of such a nature as to cause Eleazar to act to stay the plague among those peoples, in the matter of the entity's associations with the Midianite woman.

In the experience, we find that the entity in the early portions was SO WELL thought of as to be called a prince among his peoples—a judge, a counselor to his brethren—among those who were chosen as leaders. Yet the entity allowed self-indulgence, self-gratification, to so overcome all of those purposes, all of those longings of so many, as for the entity to do that which brought (even for the moment's gratification) such disturbing conditions among those who sought the right way.

Then, in thy experiences of the present day, choose thou rather God's way. Take Him, His principles, His directing influence into account, as ye counsel with those of thy brethren, those of thy neighbors. And who is thy neighbor? He to whom ye may be an aid, a help today—whether he be in the chair beside thee or upon the other side of the globe—*he* is thy neighbor.

So live, then, as to present thy own body a living sacrifice, as ye did unknowingly in that experience; for ye stood BETWEEN destruction of life; giving thy life, even in such an act; not purposefully. But PURPOSEFULLY NOW, in intent of mind and heart and soul, ye MUST do GOOD; and not "do others" in the way that brings discouragement, disheartening, discouraging forces or disturbances. (2052–1)

The subject of this reading was a thirty-six-year-old New York attorney. In a subsequent reading, the young lawyer asked for guidance pertaining to his marital problems. He had lost interest in his wife and wanted to marry another woman. He claimed he loved both women, but in different ways, and did not want to hurt either of them.

The reading gave specific advice, and also revealed this was a karmic situation arising from that Old Testament experience. His present wife had also been his wife then, and the "other woman" had been his Moabite sexual partner.

As the entity innately has experienced, these individuals represent a definite activity taken by the entity in its experience in the earth plane among the princes —or the prince of his peoples in that experience in

240

which there was allowed self-indulgence, self-gratification, owing to the beauty physically of that individual who now would appear PHYSICALLY superior to that other duty and obligation which is a part of the entity's present experience.

And to allow such influence in the present to cause the discarding, the irreparable activity, would bring not only degradation but a continued consciousness of wrongdoing, and fear would creep in. And, so far as the mental and spiritual life of the entity is concerned, it would prove degrading to the entity. . . .

As regarding spiritual and MENTAL conditions, there is only ONE course for the entity, and that is to discard ANY relationships with [Mistress] other than of a purely helpful nature from the social angle.

There needs to be the closer relationships with the entity whom THIS body, THIS entity so belittled in that experience in which there were the needs for the priest to disregard the laws and to stay the plague of self-indulgence among those peoples.

Thus, putting away that individual who caused these will be for the betterment of self, for the development of self and that individual, as well as building for those relationships which may bring spiritual, mental, AND material blessings to the entity through the closer relationship with [Wife] who was the companion in that experience.

In analysing these conditions—to be sure, entanglements have come about, but these must be settled within self. Just as the consciousness has caused uncertainty, so will the correct spiritual and mental decision bring harmony and peace—and give BETTER activities in the experience of this entity . . . (2052-3)

In his communications with Edgar Cayce, the young man related that his wife had been unfaithful to him. Cayce felt, in the light of the above reading, that his wife carried a hidden urge to defy and hurt him, just as he had disgraced and humiliated her when he fornicated with the Moabite woman, breaking the law of Moses which forbids associations with any outside the tribe of Israel. The lawyer also described that his wife's love was in the form of dependency on him. This was exactly the kind of love he needed, Cayce advised. By having the proper attitude of love and protectiveness toward her, he would be able to make up for his past experience with her.

It was also pointed out to him that any sexual relationships with the other woman, whether legally married to her or not, would always carry with it a consciousness of sin. In the subconscious mind of both, there would always be the memory of their being used as an example of immorality.

Another Example

Perhaps more than Zimri and Cozbi were slain. This reading speaks of actions by Eleazar, the father of Phineas. The entity sought to learn about a companion who had been destroyed, and gained a concept of morality, the reading states, "experienced by few."

Before that the entity was in that land when there were the journeyings of a chosen people to the land of promise.

In those experiences when there was the full destruction of the Midianites with the activities in a portion of the land the entity was in the household of those in authority—in the name then Heloise. The entity sought to know all of those happenings to those that had attempted to hinder, as well as the outcome of the destruction of a companion with the Israelites by Eleazar.

These have brought, do bring a concept of relationships in morality to the entity in a manner that is experienced by few. These, though, make for abilities of the entity to write, or to draw conclusions from the happenings that might be applied in the experience of many, if the entity were to apply such in those directions. (3345-1)

War on Midian

The wrath of Moses was kindled against the Midianites, and he ordered their complete destruction. Only the virgin women and small female children were spared. The material gain which Balaam received from Balak gave him only short pleasure. He is listed among the dead in the ensuing campaign (Numbers 31:8).

Edgar Cayce's Bible class commentary follows:

"The Midianites were almost entirely destroyed. The young ones, who could be trained as servants, were kept. All the older ones, who might lead others astray, were put to death. This was the result of their attempt to undermine the morals of Israel. The way the Midianites lived, and the means they resorted to, made all this necessary.

"Even before he left Midian, Moses was told the day would come when all those who were not then serving the Lord would be destroyed. The same is true today. Any nation, any group of people that utterly disregards God will someday be destroyed.

"Apparently it was not possible for Israel to be in the world but not of it, as Jesus tells us to be. God has always recognized man's weaknesses. The opportunity to reach God is constantly given to man, but if man continually disregards it, then the natural laws of cause and effect will wipe him out and force him to begin all over again. Physical destruction is merciful in this sense. The Midianites not only disregarded their opportunities to get closer to God, but they became a stumbling block to the elect."

In this reading, Cayce counsels a former Midianite in the ways of Israel:

Before that we find the entity was in the land when there was the passing of the peoples known as the Hebrews through the wilderness.

There we find the entity was among the daughters of Midian, and acquainted with and in sympathy with those activities of those peoples in many ways. Yet with the destructive forces that came about through wars (as is manifested in the adverse forces of Mars), we find that wrath, anger in the minds of others has driven the entity oft to do and be in the present—as through THOSE experiences—that which it of itself chose not, because of the FEAR as created by the wrath of many forms in the experiences of those with whom the entity was thrown.

The name then was Abijah.

In the present experience, again we find the abilities in many directions, the abilities of comprehension, the activities in which knowledge may easily become a part of the entity's experience. The application is not always so easy. But if the entity will turn to those forces and influences from which all power arises— knowing the SOURCES of that ye believe, as WELL as what ye believe—then ye may be enabled to enact and to carry ON in a way and manner that will become more self-assertive, not as with selfish motives, but for the good of the PURPOSE for which the entity seeks expression and manifestation in and throughout this experience. (1752-1)

A Michigan housewife was told she had been a Midianite and yet was not slain:

Before that we find the entity was in the Holy Land when those peoples were journeying there. The entity was among the Midianites who consorted with the peoples led by Moses and Joshua.

There was a reckoning, as others were in authority.

Yet the entity found that which answered to a something within and gained through that experience, for
being spared to journey with the sons of Manasseh
into the Holy Land.

The name then was Jeluen. (5231-1)

Apparently 1752 and 523 were among the 32,000
Midianite virgins who were spared. (Numbers 31:35)

The Death of Moses

Why was Moses not allowed to enter the Promised
Land? This question has occupied many minds. The
clairvoyant readings of Edgar Cayce suggest that it
was a natural result from cause and effect law.

This interpretation is based upon the answer which
Cayce gave when asked which material would best
parallel the "A Search for God" Study Group work.

The Bible is the best parallel, especially the admonition
by Moses after he had finished all of his own egotism
and had come to realize that there was not to be the
experience in self for the enjoying of that which had
been builded, owing to that weakness of selfishness.
That's the last chapters of Deuteronomy, of 30th on.
(262-100)

Apparently Moses knew for most of the forty years that
he would not enter the Promised Land. (See Deuteronomy 1:37, Numbers 20:12, and Deuteronomy 3:
23-27) By the end of his life, Moses was able to realize
and accept that it was something within him, his own
selfishness, which prevented him from entering.

He expressed two great indications of spiritual maturity
—honesty with self, and detachment from results.

Chapter 30 of Deuteronomy indicates the consciousness which Moses had evolved. The key passage is
found in verses 11-14 (King James translation):

For this commandment which I command thee this day, it is not hidden from thee, neither is it far off.

It is not in heaven, that thou shouldest say, Who shall go up for us to heaven, and bring it to us, that we may hear it, and do it?

Neither is it beyond the sea, that thou shouldest say, Who shall go over the sea for us, and bring it unto us, that we may hear it, and do it?

But the word is very nigh unto thee, in thy mouth, and in thy heart, that thou mayest do it. (Deuteronomy 30:11-14)

In this reading Cayce draws a lesson for Moses' development:

. . . and yet there have been and are periods when confusions arise and when some individual expression has drawn off the entity to seek its activity, even as Moses turned aside to see the bush on fire and yet was not consumed.

So the entity, as in Moses, finds itself slow in making comprehension until he had been through those experiences of even being in the presence of the divine, having given to man the outline of the law, and of how man in his relationship to God, in his relationship to his fellowman, in his relationship to himself could say, as must the entity learn, "Say not who will descend from heaven to bring a message, for lo! the whole law is expressed, is manifested, is indicated within one's own consciousness." For the body is indeed the temple of the living God and He hath promised to meet thee there.

Open thy consciousness and let it ever be . . . not merely in words, but in purposes, of hopes, of desires . . . (5276-1)

The inwardness and great significance of this verse is further discussed in the following.

246

Thus, as the lawgiver interpreted, "Lo, He is within thee." Man's discerning of that he would worship, then, is within self; how that he, the individual entity, makes manifest in his dealings daily with his fellowmen that God is, and that the individual entity is—in body, in mind, in soul—a witness of such; and thus he loveth, he treateth his brother as himself.

Such an admonition has in man's interpretation oft put God, the mighty, the Lord, as far away. And yet he recognizes, if he accepts this admonition of the lawgiver, that He is within self.

This is more clearly demonstrated and interpreted in the words of the Master himself, "In my Father's house are many mansions," many consciousnesses, many stages of enfoldment, of unfoldment, of blessings, of sources. And yet God has not willed that any soul should perish, but has with every temptation, every trial prepared a way of escape—or a way to meet same; which is indicated here by the Creator, the Maker of heaven and earth and all that in them be. (2879-1)

The Body of Moses

A very enigmatic verse appears in the New Testament concerning the death of Moses:

Yet Michael, the archangel, when contending with the devil about the body of Moses, did not dare to bring railing accusation against him, but said, The Lord rebuke thee. (Jude 1:9)

The war over Moses' body is an illustration of the real conflict that goes on within the soul.

While there may be in the experience of the entity much of earthly fame, much of earthly fortune, these abused will turn again and demand flesh for flesh, and

247

these become—as it were with [Michael]—disputing with Satan over the body of Moses. (1406-1)

Shortly after physical death, the soul undergoes a period of transition, or "inter-between" state, in which there is the movement from a material to a spiritual consciousness. In the after-life, the Cayce readings declare, our three-dimensional consciousness is absorbed by our subconscious mind which becomes the conscious mind of the soul.

In the subconscious mind there are programmed in psychic patterns the energies which have prompted all our thoughts, acts, and deeds while on earth. "To be absent from the body is to be present with the god (or gods) you have worshipped," the readings both promised and warned.

Moses was present with the two great forces he expressed in his life. The Devil represents the energies of self-will and egoism which would retard his development and hold his consciousness in the earth. Michael represents the protection and defense inherent in Moses' spiritual development, and would aid the soul in its evolution in new dimensions of consciousness.

The warring over (or within) the body of Moses was to determine the direction his soul would go in its experiences in the after-life.

Q-4 Are angels and archangels synonymous with that which we call laws of the universe; if so, explain and give an example.
A-4 They are as the laws of the universe; as is Michael the lord of the Way; *not* the Way but the lord of the Way, hence disputed with the influence of evil as to the way of the spirit of the teacher or director in his entrance through the outer door. (5749-3)

No doubt the symbolic clash between Michael and the

devil was over each soul, but people who are leaders are especially subject to these contending forces.

Q-8 Why is Edgar Cayce surrounded by such wrong vibrations and entities in this great work?
A-8 For there has been the continued battle with those forces as Michael fought *with* over the body of Moses. He that leads, or *would* direct, is continually beset by the forces that *would* undermine. He that endureth to the end shall wear the crown. He that aideth in upbuilding shall be entitled to that that he builds in his experience. He that faltereth, or would hinder, shall be received in the manner as he hinders. (2897-4)

Moses demonstrated a way, and it was the best which had been shown. But it was not perfect—for selfishness had entered. Consequently, there were questions. And whenever a question is present, Satan is at hand.

Cayce saw in the life of Jesus a demonstration of the perfect Way, and one in which there was no question.

This counsel to a Jewish philanthropist who had interested himself in Cayce's Christ-oriented philosophy indicates Michael will defend all those who give service through a spiritual ideal.

Even as Michael in the way defended from the wicked one the body of the lawgiver of thine people, mine people, even as this mighty Lord of thy Way defended him may he defend thee in the ways thou goest, if thou will only keep thy hand in the Master's hand. (900-428)

The Bones of Moses

The bones of Joseph were carried with the Israelites until the passing of Joshua, and served as a focus for protection and inspiration. Yet the burial place of Moses was never revealed. The people were not allowed to know this. They would have made a shrine of his tomb, and thus jeopardized the whole purpose of his life. Moses had dedicated himself to the worship of God as *Spirit*. At the tomb, the people would be worshipping Moses—the man—rather than the Spirit which inspired his teaching, enlightened his mind, and directed his life.

The Promise in the Christ is "That where I am there ye may be also." This is the Promised Land for all who seek that estate we had with the Father before the world was. True understanding is found in knowing we are at-one with God.

Hence, the individual who aided man in setting forth laws, rules, or regulations—or who is known as the lawgiver—gave expression to that which, if it is wholly understood in the consciousness of an individual, puts before him all the problems and yet the answers to same, day by day.

Then, as he gave, it is not who will descend from heaven to bring you a message, or who will come from over the seas or from without to make you aware; but lo, the whole answer is within thy own consciousness. For, as ye become aware of this in thy relationships, there is the realization within self of that spiritual awareness which may enable self to DO that which is ever the constructive exercising of the will in materiality, for: today there is set before thee good and evil life and death; choose thou.

That factor of the spiritual self, or of the soul (the will), then enables the individual to cooperate with that spirit, that truth, that fact which has ever been set before man: "If ye will be my son, I will be thy God"; "If ye call, I will hear"; "Behold, I stand at the door and knock; I will enter, if ye ask."

Then, these are not mere sayings! They are FACTS, truths, life itself! but the individual is not made aware of same through the material things nor material-mindedness; rather through spiritual-mindedness, as to purposes and activities of the soul in its lessons, its tenets that it has carried through its expressions in the earth. (1797–3)

The Relevance and Significance of the Phenomena and Philosophy of EDGAR CAYCE Today

In one reading Edgar Cayce was asked what the highest psychic realization was for man. He answered, "That God speaks directly to the sons of men."

Stated simply, the great significance of Edgar Cayce is that for thousands of people he has made this realization possible.

The most important discovery an individual can make is that God is within. Like Jesus, we all may know "I and the Father are One."

The Bible is one of the most important legacies given to men.

In no other work or record do we have such a vision of the potential and possibilities of which man is capable. The Cayce readings really only amplify and interpret the basic themes, assumptions, and promises expressed in Scripture.

What greater promise could come from any teacher or leader than the one given by Jesus, "Greater things than these I do, ye shall do because I go to my Father."

Cayce showed, through the example of his life, how this promise might be fulfilled.

Those who knew him remember Edgar Cayce not as a great psychic who possessed a wide range of paranormal sensibilities. The enduring impression was of a deeply spiritual man committed to the path of brotherly love, self-sacrifice, and service, a man infused with confidence and trust in his Creator.

The quest for self-realization and self-development

speaks strongly to modern man. The Cayce readings are unique in their vision. There is a cosmic dimension to all men, and a practical means to obtain it. If Jesus was perfect, it was because it is the potential of all men to become perfect.

Edgar Cayce lived as a disciple of Christ's, whose life reflected his belief in the promises of his master. Although hundreds came to listen to his words, and many thousands were given counsel and advice, and his psychic gifts far surpassed that of any living person, Edgar Cayce gently reminded them that they all had equal access to the Source from which his gifts arose.

Equally significant in the Cayce philosophy is that nowhere is the development of psychic power a primary goal. Living in unity and harmony with God's Laws and raising the Christ-consciousness within are the central objectives. The *fruits* of the Spirit—patience, kindness, long-suffering, tolerance, sensitivity to the needs of others —are valued more highly than the *gifts*, which include clairvoyance, telepathy, aura-reading, and other forms of psychic phenomena.

Psychic development, the readings show, is the natural outgrowth of spiritual development.

The great emphasis in the Cayce readings is on personal application of spiritual truths. Only by living the truths which are presented to us can we ever experience, understand, or evaluate them.

In a restless, questioning age, when many individuals are seeking new values and life styles, Cayce points us to the Bible, this central piece of literature which bespeaks where the source of our strength, our health, and well-being can be found, and gives us the key for its interpretation.

To understand it, we must live it.

What could be more relevant and significant today than the incentive the Cayce philosophy provides for testing out that truth which Jesus taught—that "we are gods," made in His Image.

RECOMMENDED READING

Trilogy of Creation by Eula Allen, ARE Press.
  Before the Beginning: A Study of Spiritual Creation, 1963.
  River of Time: A Study of the Physical Creation, 1965.
  You Are Forever: A Study of Man's Struggle to Overcome Materiality, 1966.

My Years with Edgar Cayce: The Story of Gladys Davis Turner by Mary E. Carter, Harper & Row, 1972.

Edgar Cayce's Story of Karma by Mary Ann Woodward, Berkley, 1972.

Aaron, 154, 162, 169, 170, 183, 192, 214, 219, 223, 231
    breastplate of, 208-10
Abarther, 201
Abatha, 155
Abazeal, 228
Abel, 51
    murder of, 57, 61, 67, 125
Abiathar, 218
Abigal, 187
Abihu, 211-13, 217-18, 228
Abijah, 244
Abimilech, 112-14
Abiram, 224
Abraham (Abram), 103-19
    Isaac and, 124-26
    Lot saved by, 121-23
    Melchizedek and, 103, 105-6, 109
    Sarah and, 110, 111, 113-19, 124
Adah, 63
Adam
    Fall of, xxiii, 45-54
    first reference to, 37-38, 39
    formation of, 27-29
    naming of animals by, 37
    subsequent incarnations of, 36
Adamic race, 27n
    five lines of, xxii-xxiii, 32-36
    reason for development of, 55
Adultery in seventh commandment, 200
Ajlon, 227
Akashic Record, 11
Allen, Eula, 47
Amalekites, 192
Amillius, 36, 39
Andes, the, 33, 35
Angels as laws of the universe, 248
Ani, 76
Animals
    in Ark, 82
    forming and naming of, 37
    speaking by, 237
Apple, the, 37, 45-47
Araaraatt, 71
Archangels, 247-48
Ark, the, 82-88
Ark of the Convention, 203, 205, 208, 218
Arthritis, healing from, 136n
Asaph, xxiii
Ashbahel, 226
Ashua, 213
As-sen-ni, 67
Association for Research and Enlightenment, Inc., xiin, xv
Astrology, xvi

Atlantis, xv, xxiv, xxv, 11-12, 222
    Adam in, 32
    destruction of, 75-76
    exodus from, 91
    records of, 71-72, 77, 82
Automatons, 66n, 74

Baal-pero, 238
Babel, Tower of, 57, 97-101, 177
Babylonian mythology, "Tablets of Destiny" in, 209
Balaam, 235-38, 243
Balak, 235-38, 243
Belial, see Sons of Belial
Beloi, 111
Benjamin, 132
Beth-Korah, 194
Bezaleel, 192
Bible, the
    Cayce readings and, 253
    literal interpretation of, 65
    as pattern of mental unfoldment, 177-78
    versions of, xii
Bilhah, 131
Bithiah, 157
Body
    gold as connecting link between mind and, 34
    purification of, in Temple of Sacrifice, 92-94
    as temple, 30, 201, 246
Boils, plague of, 173
"Born again," 179-80
Breath, Holy, 28-29
Burning bush, 160-62, 163, 191, 197, 246

Cain, 51
    as result of Fall, 47-48
    murder of Abel by, 57, 61, 67, 125
    Sons of, see Sons of Belial
Caleb, 220, 222
"Calling," 163-64
Cambell, Thomas, 79
Carpathia, 33, 34
Cayce Hospital, closing of, 120
Ceclia, 169
Children of the Light, 6
    See also Sons of God
Chosen people, 24
Christ, see Jesus
Churchward (author), 170
Coats of skin, 61-62
Consciousness, 25
    three dimensions of, xxiv
1 Corinthians (epistle)

257

1 Corinthians (Continued)
3:15, 120*n*
10:13, 124
Cozbi, 239, 242
Creation, xviii-xix, xxi-xxii, 1-19
  Cayce's analysis of days of, 13-19
  Mind and, 1-2, 25-26
  myths of, 33
Creative Energy in God's Mind, 1-2

Da, 11
Dan, tribe of, 202-3
Darkness, plague of, 174
Dathan, 224
Daughters of Men, 9-10, 66*n*
Death, soul after, 247-48
"Deep sleep" as meditation, 40
Deluge (Flood), 73-91
  Atlantis' destruction by, 75-76
  Enoch's warning of, 69-70, 71
  worldwide myths about, 81
Deuteronomy
  1:37, 245
  3:23-27, 245
  30:11-14, 245-46
  32:8, 57
Devil, the, 55, 248
  as Serpent, 46-48
  as spiritual rebellion, xxii, 2, 3
Dinah, 135-36
Divine Awareness, xxi-xxii
Divine Image, xxii, 8-9

Earth, subduing of, 26-27
Eden, *see* Garden of Eden
Edomites, passage of Israelites prevented by, 232-34
Ego, development of, 60-63
Egypt, 35, 91-94
  can be left at any time, 176-77
  Joseph in, 141-49
  Moses in, 151-75
  See also Pharaoh
Eijalu, 203
Elded, 202
Eleasiah, 194
Eleazar, 218, 239, 242
Electricity, Mount Sinai as charged with, 197
Eliab, 224
Elijah, 109, 153
Elisha, 79, 109
Elzjah, 237
Endocrine system, 116, 127, 200
Enoch, 36, 56, 69-72, 107
  records of Atlantis preserved by, 77
Enos, 56
Esau, 134
Essenes, xiii, 109
Esther (book), 135

Ethiopian woman, Moses' marriage to, 219, 223
Eve
  creation of, 40-43
  daughters of, 68
  as Mary, 50, 53
  temptation of, 44-50
Evolution, 1, 2, 5-6
  of animals, 37-38
Exodus, 151-212
  1:11, 179
  2:5, 66
  2:11-12, 157
  2:15-22, 160
  3:21-22, 145
  4:10-15, 163
  6:9, 177
  7:8-11, 169
  8:1-15, 172
  8:30-32, 173
  9:1-7, 173
  9:8-12, 173
  9:13-35, 173
  9:16, 172
  10:1-20, 174
  10:21-28, 174
  12:29-30, 174
  12:35-36, 145
  15:2, 181
  15:20-21, 181
  16:2-3, 183
  17:10, 192
  18:25-26, 194
  19:5, 193
  19:9-11, 195
  19:16, 195
  19:18-20, 196
  24:13, 154
  24:14, 192
  24:25-27, 202
  25:17-18, 206
  25:21-22, 205
  26:1, 206
  26:30, 208
  26:31-33, 203
  28:29, 209
  31:2, 192
  32:1, 196
  33:7, 154
Ezakiai, [?], 156
Ezekiel, 199

Fiery serpents, 234-35
First-born, slaying of, 172, 174-76
First Consciousness, xxi
Flood, the, *see* Deluge
"Forbidden fruit," *see* Apple, the
Frogs, plague of, 172

Garden of Eden, xxv, 29-31, 36, 66
  Eve's temptation in, 45-50
Genesis, xv, xviii-xix
  1, 1-19
  1:1, xviii

Genesis (Continued)
  1:2, xxi
  1:3, 7-8, 12, 13
  1:27, 8, 17
  1:29, 62
  2, 21-43
  2:6, 21
  2:9, 36
  2:10, 31
  2:11, 34
  2:15-17, 36
  2:19, 36, 39
  3, 45-54
  3:7-8, 49
  3:15, 54n, 73
  3:21, 61
  4, 55-72
  4:19, 131
  4:19-24, 68
  4:20, 64
  4:22, 64, 67
  4:26, 56
  5, 77
  6:1-2, 9
  6:2, 66n
  6:5-6, 74
  6:6, 78
  6:9, 79
  9, 100
  9:12-17, 89-91
  9:20, 88
  9:21-25, 81
  11, 97-101
  12, 113
  14, 109
  14:18-20, 103
  15, 115
  15:12-15, 160
  15:14, 145
  16, 115
  17:3-8, 121
  18, 119
  18:17-33, 122
  19:1, 15, 16, 119
  19:20, 121
  19:26, 119
  19:31-35, 121
  20, 113, 14
  23, 110
  25:23, 127
  30:25-43, 134
  32:24-28, 138
  34, 135
  35:22, 131
  37, 132
  41:51-52, 147
  42, 142
  42:21, 147
  49, 131
Genius, nature of, 65
Gershonites, 226-27
Giants reported by Moses' spies, 219
Gizeh, construction of Great Pyramid at, 70-72

Gobi, 33, 35
God
  Beginning and, xviii-xix, xxi-xxii, 1-19
  companionship desired by, 37
  fragmenting of, 60
  as love, xxii
  Moses' re-identification of, 152-53
  as One, 51-52
  See also Divine Image
Gold as connecting link between mind and body, 34
Gomorrah, *see* Sodom and Gomorrah
Good Shepherd, 26
Graven images, 198-99
Great Pyramid, construction of, 70-72

Hagar, 115-16, 118-19
Hailstorm, plague of, 173-74
Hall, Manly, 70
Ham, 81, 100
Hatherpsut, 158-59, 210
Havilah (land), 34
Hebrews (epistle), *7:17*, 107
Heliopolis (On), 145-46
Heloise, 242
Henriettah, 211
Hep-Su-Tun, 185
Hermes, 70-72
Heth, 110, 111
Hittites, 83
Holy Land, God's promise of, 220
Holy of Holies, 203, 204, 207
Homosexuality as due to pre-Adamic experience, 11
Human nature, 166-67
Hur, 188, 192-94

Immaculate conception (Virgin Birth), 59
  of Eve, 42
  of Mary, 50
India, 33, 35
Intuition, 41
Isaac, 109, 111
  Abraham and, 124-26
  birth of twins to, 127
Isaiah, 233
Ishmael, 110, 112, 116-19
Israel, 28
  meaning of term, 220
  renaming of, 138
Ithamar's son, 214
Izhar, 224

Jabal, 63
Jacob, 109
  friend of, 133-35
  renaming of, 138
  Reuben and, 131-32

Jacob's ladder, 136-38
James (epistle), *1:13*, 124
Japeth, 84-89
Japin, 221
Jarael, 188-89
Jared, 233
Jehovah, meaning of word, 161-62
Jeluen, 245
Jericho, 235
Joshua, 36, 107, 154
Jesus Christ
    on being born again, 179-80
    death on cross of, 235
    as first and last Adam, xxiii, 28, 52-54
    knows he will be Savior, 50
    Light in, 2, 7, 13
    Peter and, 104, 105, 115
    Sermon on the Mount of, 198
    three primary appearances of, 107
    Way demonstrated in, 249
Jethro, 160, 168, 191-92
Jeurepth, 101
Jewish refugees, 165
Joan of Arc, 168
Job (book), written by Melchizedek, 22, 108, 153
Jochabed, 155, 156, 214
John (gospel), 2
    2:21, 30
    8:3-11, 130
    8:56-58, 103
    10:34, xi
    14:30, 45
John, Revelation of, *see* Revelation of St. John
Joseph, 36, 107, 134, 141-50
    as first physical incarnation of Adam, 132, 141
Josephus, *Antiquities of the Jews*, 71
Joshua, xix, 36, 107, 187-91, 220, 222, 229, 249
    giants to be slain by, 219
    Moses and, 153-54
Joshua (book), *24:15*, 30
Jubal, 64
Judah, 129
Judah, tribe of, 215
Jude (epistle)
    1:9, 247
    1:11, 238
    1:14, 56

Kaballah, Hermes linked with Enoch in, 71
Keturah, 191
Killing
    by Phineas, in name of God, 239
    in sixth commandment, 200
Kohath, 224
Korah, 187, 212, 223-30
Kotapet, 142

Laban, 134
Lamb "slain before the foundation of the world," 32
Lamech, 68, 69, 131
Lapeth, 87
Laws of the universe, angels as, 248
Leah, 131
Leakey, Richard, xxiv
Lemuria, 11, 35, 39
Levi, 135, 136, 193, 211, 224
Leviticus
    10:1, 212
    10:2, 213
Lice, plague of, 172
Lifespan, 77-79
Light, the, 7-8, 12-13
    as of Son of Man, 13-14
Locusts, plague of, 173-74
Lot and Lot's wife, 111, 119-22
Love, God as, xxii
Lucifer, *see* Devil, the
Luke (gospel), *2*, 52
Lust, 10, *46n*
    See also Sex

Magicians of Egypt, 169
Male-female beings, 7, 41
Man
    evolution of, 38
    rebellion of, xxi
    See also Adam; Adamic race
Manasseh, 245
Manna, 183-86
Maran, 83
Marriage, 43
    See also Sex
Mary
    as Eve, 50, 53
    Immaculate Conception of, 50
Matthew (gospel)
    16:15-16, 104
    16:22-23, 115
Meah, 237-38
Melchizedek, 36, 105-9
    Abraham and, 103, 105-6, 109
    Job written by, 22, 108, 153
    as priest, 107
Mercy seat, 205, 206-8
Meribah, 230-32
Methuselah, 77
Michael the archangel, 247-49
Midian, 160, 168, 191, 237
    Moses' war on, 243-45
Mind
    Creation and, 1-2, 25-26
    in post-Deluge era, 94-95
Miriam, 155, 156, 181, 195, 211, 214, 219, 223
Mississippi basin, 35
Mr. 257, 215-18
Moabite women, fornication with 238-42

260

Moses, xix, 38, 97, 151-251
  birth of, 154-57
  bones of, 249
  death of, 245-49
  Ethiopian woman married by,
    219, 222
  Pharaoh and, 165-75
  at Sinai, 189, 191-201
  in the wilderness, 182-91, 218-45
Mount Sinai, 189, 191-201
Mu, 11, 39, 83

Nadab, 211-18, 228
New Jerusalem, 110n
Nicodemus, 179
Nile River, 35
  changed into blood, 171
Noah, 76, 79-82, 88
  purity of generation of, 60
Numbers (book)
  10:35, 218
  11, 219
  13:33, 219
  13:31-32, 221
  14:1-3, 223
  16:5-7, 225
  16:28-32, 227
  20:2-3, 230
  20:10-11, 231
  20:12, 245
  20:14-18, 20-21, 233
  21, 235
  21:6-9, 234
  22, 235
  22:20-22, 236
  22:27-28, 237
  25:1-3, 238
  31:8, 243

Odenatus of Palmyra, 237-38
Og, 11
On (city), 145-46
On (person), 224
Opportunity, World as, 4
Oz, 11

Parents, honoring of, 200
Patience, xxiv
Paul, 164
Peleth, 224
Pelus, 88
Peter
  rebuked by Jesus, 115
  recognizes Jesus as Christ, 104,
    105
2 Peter (epistle)
  2:15, 238
  3:9, xxii
Pharaoh, 142, 148, 152
  Abraham and, 113, 114
  Moses and, 165-75
Pharaoh's daughter, 154, 155, 157,
    167
Phineas, 239

Pishon (river), 34
Plagues, the, 166, 168-76
Poseida, 75
Prayer, power of, 122-24
Pre-Adamic World, xxii, 9-13
Prodigal Son, xxii
Promised land, meaning of, 250
Psalms
  82:6, xi
  110:4, 107
Psychic development as outgrowth
    of spiritual development, 254

Ra-Ta, 70-71, 136, 210
Races, five, xxii-xxiii, 32-36
Rachel, 126, 132, 135
Rainbow after the Deluge, 89-91
Rakim, 232
Raoul, 134
Readings, Cayce's, described, xiii-
    xv
Rebekah, 126, 127
Rebellion
  Devil as, xxii, 2
  Man's, xxi
Red Sea, Moses' crossing of, 179-
    80
Reincarnation, xiv, xvi
  sons of fathers and, 199
Resurrection, reason for, 53-54
Reuben, 131-32, 224
Reul, 160
Revelation of St. John, xv, xix-xx,
    205
  2:14, 238
  3:14-16, 160
  11:3, 205
  13:8, 32
  21, 110n
  22:2, 66
Rezepatha, 84, 80
River, four-headed, 31
Ruth (book), 135

Sabbath, 199-200
Sacrifice
  of Isaac, 124-26
  nature of, 63
  Temple of, 92-94
Sahara Desert, 35
Samuel, 109, 153
Sarah, 110, 111, 113-19, 124
Satan, see Devil, the
Saul, King, 133
School of Prophets, 109, 153
Seances, 42
Segualar, 203
Sermon on the Mount, 198
Serpent, the, 46-48, 73
  fiery, 234-35
  See also Devil, the
Seth, 51, 59, 71, 133
  children of, 64, 81

Sex
　creation of, 40-43
　"forbidden fruit" as, 45-47
　ideals and purposes of, 126-29
　and Israelites in the wilderness,
　　238-42
　Sons of Belial and, 59
Shalmahr, 190
Shebeth, 193
Shechem, 135, 136
Shem, 220
Sheol, Moses' enemies consumed
　by, 228-29
Shittim, 238
Shulzar, 230
Shushan, 195
Simeon, 135, 136
Sidiptu, 158
Sinai, see Mount Sinai
Sodom and Gomorrah, 119-23, 177
Solar System, creation of, 16-17
Sons of Belial (Sons of Cain), 49,
　57-59, 67
　automatons and, 74
Sons of Darkness, 6
Sons of God (Sons of Adam)
　in Amilius, 36, 38
　entry into earth of, 23-27, 31
Sons of the Law of One, 59, 63,
　73, 91-92, 222
　See also Sons of God
Sons of Man, 10
Soul
　animal associations of, 39
　after death, 247-48
　evolution of, 1, 2
　as sexless, 41
　See also Divine Image
Sour grapes, 199
Space, xxiii-xxiv
Spence, Lewis, 76n
Sphinx, 91
Spirit
　Adamic race as expression of,
　　55
　male-female union as means of
　　return to Oneness of, 42-43
　origin of all things in, 1
　psychic development and, 254
　water as first materialization of,
　　22
Stones in Aaron's breastplate, 208-
　10
Strange fire, 212-15, 228
Sugru, Tom, xv

Tabernacle, 201-5, 208
Tahi, 156
Tamar, 129
Tanai, 155
Teheru, Princess, 148
Tekla, 147
Temah, 112

Temple, the, 201-5
　body as, 30, 201, 246
Ten, symbology of, 206
Ten Commandments, receiving of,
　198-201
Tep-Lepan, 149
Terahe, 112
Thanksgiving, lesson of, 186-87
Thessalonica, 143
Thummin, 210-12
"Things" (automatons), 66n, 74
Thought-forms, end of, 89-91
Time, xxiii-xxiv
　as relative concept, 5
Torah, 153
Trances, Cayce's, xiii
Tree of Knowledge, 30, 36
Tree of Life, 30, 65-67
Tubal-Cain, 64, 67-69
Tuesday Night Bible Class, ix, xv-
　xvii
Two, symbology of, 205

Ur, 111, 115
Ural Mountains, 35
Urim and Thummin, 210-12

Vegetarian diet, 62
Velikovsky, Dr. Immanuel, 185
Versions of the Bible, xii
Virgin Birth, see Immaculate con-
　ception
Vocations, first practitioners of,
　63-65

Wakefield, Norman, xxiv
Water
　as beginning of life, 14-15, 171-
　　72
　as first materialization of spirit,
　　22
　from the rock, 230-31
White Brotherhood, 71
Wilderness, the, 182-91, 211-12,
　214-15, 218-45
　Isaiah and, 233
Woman, creation of, 40-43
Word, the, 26
　See also Mind
Worlds in Collision (Velikovsky),
　185

Yucatan, 33, 91

Zephaniah, 182
Zeruba, 168
Zerva, 144
Zeta-Elda, 176
Zillah, 64
Zimri, 239, 242
Zin, wilderness of, 182-91, 211-15,
　214-15, 218-45
Zipohar, 224
Zipporah, 191